Advance Praise for

# *Ready to Teach?*

Deborah and Janis capture a combination of research, personal experience, and the experiences of their colleagues in an easy-to-read, practical guide for beginning teachers. This book brings to life the realities of what teachers face and how to think and respond in ways that are healthy and sustainable. The authors have successfully created classroom cultures and student relationships that allowed students to learn and succeed.

—**Judy Flores,** Shasta County Superintendent of Schools

In *Ready to Teach?* Hawthorne and Upshaw pick up where your university training left off. Their practical and proven advice will save the new teacher hours of time and bottles of aspirin while improving the quality of their early years. I wish I had been able to start my teaching career by standing on the shoulders of such giants.

—**Brad Fulton,** California Middle School Educator of the Year

# READY to TEACH?

# READY to TEACH?

## Tips & Tales

### FOR THE

## New Elementary Teacher

Janis Hawthorne and Deborah Upshaw

*Ready to Teach? Tips and Tales for the New Elementary School Teacher*

Copyright © 2024
Janis Hawthorne and Deborah Upshaw

Published by 2 Plumes Press



Editor: Gail Fallen
Publishing and Design Services: MelindaMartin.me
ISBN: 979-8-218-30842-1(paperback), 979-8-218-30843-8 (epub)

To my many teacher friends whose love and
laughter sustained me through the years.

—Debbie


To all of the kids who made me love teaching
—and Damien too.

—Janis


Special mention to our friend and principal,
Brien McCall, who had the wisdom to hire us.

# Contents

# Preface

Sitting among a group of thirty or more eager, smiling teachers dressed to impress at the district's "new teacher" training workshop, we sat down next to each other by chance. We were delighted to find out that we would be fourth-grade-level partners. Little sparks of friendship ignited as we discovered the amazing commonalities we shared.

We both entered the profession after raising our three children. Our husbands even shared the same name, "Mitch," necessitating the terms "my Mitch" or "your Mitch" in our everyday conversations. We recognized how simpatico we were early on, but we never dreamed we would be coauthoring a book.

We entered our teaching careers with our eyes wide open. Both of us had substantial experience working in the classroom as teacher's aides. We *knew* that teaching required multifaceted skills and carried many responsibilities. However, there was a big chasm between our perceptions and reality.

That first year, we were so grateful to have one another. We'd meet together daily to design lessons, to report successes, and, perhaps most importantly, to vent our frustrations common to the new-teacher experience.

At other times we would recount an extraordinary experience or share an epiphany. These conversations on the fly always ended with, "We never learned this in credentialing! We should write a book!"

Naturally, our first recourse was to read books written for beginning teachers. However, we continued to encounter problematic situations in our classrooms that weren't addressed in these books. As we found ways of navigating our own solutions, we started writing them down. Before long, we believed we had something of value to share with novice teachers.

Our book is a collaborative effort. By joining our two voices, we were able to distill the essential ideas that will provide new teachers with what they will need to acquire staying power. Therefore, we wrote this book from the first-person point of view for simplicity.

The tips and tales we share are a compilation of our experiences and those of other teachers.

# Introduction

You have chosen one of the most gratifying professions possible. Yet because of the countless challenges, there is a good chance you may not last beyond five years. Did you know that the teaching profession has one of the highest attrition rates in the US?

One of the major reasons new teachers walk out the door is due to stress, both physical and emotional. In addition to the enormous amount of pressure put on you for your students to perform well, you will face an extraordinary workload and numerous other responsibilities.

Hope we didn't scare you off, because the practical advice you will discover in this book will inspire you to change your focus, not your career. This is the book we searched for when we first started. We present a realistic portrayal of the pitfalls of teaching while at the same time offering hints, tips, and positive suggestions for dealing with them or avoiding them altogether. We outline explicit strategies that you can put to use immediately. We share what worked for us. You will gain a clear picture of the demands of teaching and ways of managing them. Nothing counters anxiety more than preparedness.

We hope that our insights and advice may help you to join the ranks of men and women who have committed their lives to a satisfying and lasting teaching career.

## CHAPTER 1

# You're Hired!
# What's Next?

You've been celebrating with friends and family after just having signed your first teaching contract. However, your euphoria may dissolve into feelings of inadequacy and nervousness when you tackle the logistics of setting up your classroom.

You may find yourself standing in the midst of a nicely furnished, abundantly supplied workspace. If so, congratulations! You have just won the new teacher *lotto*, and you are in rare company!

> **Don't Assume That You'll Have
> All the Essentials, Even the Furniture!**

It is quite possible that you may be escorted into a room with four bare walls needing paint; a shabby, pink-and-blue metal teacher's desk; metal cabinets from the seventies era in one corner; mismatched student desks and chairs; and antiquated textbooks on the shelves. Your only recourse may be to do what thousands of other beginners do: use leftovers and hand-me-downs from other teachers.

While the university does a decent job of preparing educators for teaching curriculum, nothing is said about how much support they may or may not receive in setting up a classroom.

As a student teacher, what you see in your master teacher's classroom are usually many years' worth of acquired furnishings, wall decor, and other classroom embellishments. Just as a young married couple may hold as their standard for their new home the house that their parents have spent a lifetime putting together, the tendency for a new teacher is to expect to duplicate the environment that a seasoned teacher has spent years creating. Don't fall into that trap!

"I had no cupboards or shelves at all," sixth-grade teacher Mrs. Berdinski recalled. "I pillaged metal cabinets and computer tables from abandoned classrooms at my site. In addition, I spent my own money to purchase a four-drawer file cabinet, bookshelves, and a horseshoe table to use for small group instruction."

You will quickly learn that very few teachers escape the school year without dipping into their own pocket for classroom necessities.

It is imperative that you ask your school secretary or administrator how much money you will be allotted for your classroom supplies. These budgets vary from school to school. Don't rush off and purchase a new bookcase, only to find that you're already in the red! Also, check your supply room. You may find your school provides some basics.

## Needs versus Desires

Keep two separate lists: the "must haves" and the "wishes or wants." You will most likely buy the bulk of your supplies with a purchase order through your school district. However, your school may allow personal reimbursement for extraneous items, so you'll want to hang onto your receipts and always stay within your budget.

Looking back to when I first started teaching, I received $350 for classroom supplies. Little did I know that figure would look lush compared to what followed as the budget shrank smaller and smaller, year after year.

There are creative ways to maximize your spending power. For example, you can purchase crayons for $0.25 a box at the local retail store's back-to-school sale instead of ordering them through your school's "teacher account" which may cost $1.50 a box. Additionally, you can solicit donations from parents throughout the school year for items such as paper, pens, folders, glue sticks, Kleenex, etc.

Be sure to look at the numerous donor programs, such as SupplyATeacher.org, which can fill your classroom cupboards at little or no cost to you. This organization provides teachers with two boxes of essential school supplies, completely free of charge.

**You're Thinking:** *I need that cool automatic pencil dispenser I saw in the* School Tools Catalog for Teachers.

**You Need to Tell Yourself:** *I need to be vigilant about spending too much money on classroom supplies. It adds up fast!*

## Seating Suggestions

One question that must be answered is "How will I set up my students' desks or tables?"

This seemingly simple question is complex. There is no one correct seating arrangement. The factors to consider are the physical space of your room, the group dynamic of your students, and even your own personality.

- Even if you plan to change your room arrangement during the school year, it is wise to begin the year with the desks or tables facing the teacher. This minimizes distractions, allows you to monitor behavior more readily, and helps you become familiar with the students in your class.

- Desks do not have to be in traditional rows, but all chairs should face forward, at least initially. This is important for classroom management.

- Make sure your desk or table arrangement frees up all fire extinguishers and fire alarms.

- Have a strategic location ready for students with behavioral problems. I even remember a student asking me to move his desk over near the door, away from the group, because it removed distractions and helped him focus.

**Make Your Classroom Shipshape,
but Don't Go Overboard!**

While putting your desks into the desired formation, check out their condition. Custodians may or may not clean the desks or tables at your school.

Hone up on your Tom Sawyer skills and grab a few friends to help you have fun with a bucket, a sponge, and some suds. A clean environment will give you and your students a great start to the new year. In the coming months, you can train your students to keep a neat, clean area. Provide them with handy wipes to clean their desks. Students love this, and they take ownership of their personal learning space.

You'll want to temper your desire to make things perfect. There are plenty of stories of teachers being moved to a new classroom and/or a different grade level at the eleventh hour. It's always based on student enrollment, and, as most administrators will tell you, grade-level assignments are not written in stone until warm bodies are in their seats.

One teacher spent an entire summer weekend painting the student cubbies in her second-grade room. She invested many hours creating clever, colorful bulletin boards. Also, she made custom curtains for the windows. Imagine her dismay when her room was commandeered for the extra kindergarten class that materialized the first week of school.

I had a similar experience. I spent the month of July moving my fourth-grade classroom materials and furniture to a newly assigned room at the request of my principal. Ten days before the start of school, he approached me and asked, "How would you like to teach third grade in Room 1?"

I didn't have to think long: *Hmm, twenty-four kids versus thirty-two?* I thought.

I jumped at the opportunity and then found myself staying late every evening and working two weekends in a frantic effort to set up a brand-new classroom on the opposite side of campus. It was an exhausting experience, and I was desperately trying to put the finishing touches on my classroom walls and shelves right up until the evening before the first day! The payoff was seeing the smiling third graders that early September morning, knowing I was ready.

## Acquiring Teaching Materials

While you're physically preparing your classroom, you'll have to be thinking about your curriculum and lessons plans (see chapter 8).

You may be among the very fortunate to start with complete sets of teacher manuals and the accompanying students' materials.

Wyatt wasn't that lucky. He had been placed in a portable classroom with nothing more than thirty desks his first year of teaching. He had two weeks to set up his room.

"After scrounging a few bookshelves and cabinets, I naively asked my principal how to go about ordering math workbooks and manipulatives," he remembered. "With a shrug of his shoulders, he sympathetically said, 'It's sad for me to say this, but there's just no money in the budget for them right now.'"

Luckily, Wyatt's grade-level partner came to the rescue. She had extra sets of materials and was more than willing to share.

If there is a budget crunch at your school, you'll have to improvise. Other teachers at your grade level are your best resources. Also, it is likely that other sources of funding may become available during the school year. Most principals consider curriculum-related purchases a high priority, and they will go out of their way to support new teachers.

It's true, however, that money issues require rookie teachers to quickly become experts at teaching on a shoestring. You'll be tempted to accept outdated materials. You are drawn to retiring teachers like a moth to a flame knowing they are shedding years of accumulated books and supplies which may be useful. They cannot bear to throw away their cherished lessons and books and are delighted to think that their teaching legacy will endure.

It is easy to quickly saddle yourself with way too much "stuff"! Don't let your classroom cupboards become the detour from the rightful destination of the garbage can. I ended up throwing away boxes of obsolete, useless materials I acquired from retirees. With experience in the classroom, I realized that only a small percentage of these treasures were useful. Remember that you have access to more current resources and lessons online.

## Back to School

So now it's the weekend before the *first day* of school. You are surprisingly pleased with the results of your scavenging. Everything from pretty posters to the newly purchased pencil boxes makes for a pleasing, inviting classroom. You are admiring your big wall with the pretty border and heading "Our Best Work" soon to be covered with students' excellent papers. This becomes the focal point of your classroom. Students, parents, and visitors will admire this showcase.

Your tummy flutters with nerves as you sit at your desk trying to visualize each student while writing their names on nametags.

Now ponder this . . . how will you greet your students as they enter your room? Fist bump? Handshake? High five? You may want to check with your administrator as to the protocol for greeting kids at the door.

In my case, I asked the child to tell me if they wanted a hug, a high five, a fist bump, or a simple hello. Some kids are shy while others are outgoing—so let them tell you what they prefer.

The Premier Event:

It's Showtime! Opening Day!

Memorize your students' names on the first day if possible. There are many "getting to know you" games that will help you learn them. Make them fun, and the students will learn each other's names as well. This is a great way to build community so that each child feels welcome and important.

Invest a lot of time in this step. This is how you will start to create a culture in your classroom. Don't even think about curriculum on the first day. Your goal is to build positive relationships right away.

You'll be surprised how much of your first week is already locked in. There will be schoolwide assemblies welcoming the students. You'll want to take your students on a tour of the campus to orient them to well-used turf—the playground, the library, and the cafeteria.

## Battle Self-Doubt

*Take charge of your thoughts. You can do what you will with them.*

—Plato

You have spent hours and hours of your summer getting ready, but you still don't feel adequately prepared.

I certainly wasn't the only teacher who felt as if I was "pretending" to be a teacher that first day. I met teachers who said that these feelings of self-doubt persisted the entire first year.

The classroom is your stage. Standing there in front of a captive audience, you find yourself feeling like a great impostor. Who entrusted you with the education of these precious souls?

LeeAnne was ecstatic to have a teaching job for the first time in her life. Nevertheless, those unwarranted feelings of self-doubt soon crept in.

"I can remember feeling like 'someone's going to figure this out,'" she said. "I half expected the 'teacher police' to come storming through the door and lead me away in handcuffs, saying, 'You're under arrest for impersonating a teacher!'"

These feelings are normal, but with experience, these sentiments are supplanted with genuine self-assuredness and professionalism. But just be aware: It takes time.

**You're Thinking:** *I can't believe they think I'm prepared to teach this class.*

**You Need to Tell Yourself:** *This is how many first-year teachers feel. Feelings of inadequacy will eventually disappear.*

Remember this: You'll have a much better idea of what you *really need* a few months into the school year. Rather than purchasing *everything* before the school year begins, hold off until you see what you really need.

## Classroom Supplies Checklist

☑ **Necessities versus Niceties**

Pencils, binder paper, white construction paper, colored paper, crayons, colored pencils, erasers, tape, staplers and staples, glue sticks, scissors, paper clips, rubber bands, calendar, facial tissues, paper towels, and bandages

☑ **Niceties versus Necessities**

Craft tissue paper, special pens, paints, markers, dry-erase boards with dry-erase pens for students, white glue, rulers, heavy duty stapler, composition books, folders, jump ropes, Frisbees, playground balls, small refrigerator, microwave, quality desk chair, wall posters, reward stickers and prizes for younger grades

☑ **Furniture/Equipment**

Student desks or tables and chairs, a sturdy teacher's desk, worktable, bookshelves, trashcan, tubs for P. E. balls

☑ **Technology**

Check with your district about computers and technology for you and your students and classroom.

## CHAPTER 2

# Multitasking Magic

*Professionalism is knowing how to do it,*
*when to do it, and doing it.*

—Frank Tyger

Whoever said "Teachers have such great hours. They get to go home early every day" didn't know most teachers. What many people don't realize is that some teachers often stay late, work on the weekends, and take a lot of work home with them.

I remember a standout teacher, Jackie Evans, who, in the twilight of her career, taught with the enthusiasm of a rookie. It motivated me to track her down and ask her what she did to keep her battery charged year after year and avoid burnout.

What Jackie did was attend numerous workshops in her twenty-five-year career, side-stepping stagnation and burnout.

"They [the workshops] were incredible! I always took something away," she said. "The workshops were like recipes. I tweaked them to suit my taste. I was always learning."

## Burnout: The Signs

Unfortunately, by years four through ten, some teachers may lack this support and, therefore, suffer burnout. Burnout is defined by the American Institute of Stress as a cumulative process marked by mental and emotional exhaustion and withdrawal associated with increased workload and institutional stress. Some signs include fatigue, anxiety, insomnia, feelings of ineffectiveness, lack of enjoyment, depression, etc.[1] Burnout can dampen the most promising teaching career. It carries some teachers right out the door!

Consider the thoughts of third-grade teacher Brad as he awakens bright-eyed on a Monday morning.

"I must get the fraction materials ready for tomorrow's math lesson and prepare the instructional aide's reading plan for reading groups. Don't forget to call Kevin's dad and remind him to turn in the free/reduced lunch plan form. And, oh yes, I must get that purchase order submitted for the art supplies or I won't have them in time for the Thanksgiving art project. Remember to take home the writing samples to edit tonight."

Once Brad learned how to multitask and manage his time well, he became a satisfied and effective teacher. Not everyone can do this. Could one of the factors of the high attrition rate in the teaching profession be linked to this frenetic pace at which an educator is expected to perform?

How many other jobs are there that require you to know absolutely *everything* you're supposed to know on the very first day of work? Nothing in your teacher training will prepare you for the sheer volume of administrative minutia that you'll be expected to maneuver.

"It was the first week of school, and it hit me like a ton of bricks," fifth-grade teacher Amy recalled. "There was so much paperwork coming from the school office which needed to go home, be signed, and returned by the end of the week. My heart said, 'Get to know your students,' while my brain said, 'Get these papers back to the office by Friday!'"

So much is assumed! For example, you may be asked to complete and submit purchase orders to your district office online. How do you learn vendor names, funding sources, approval codes, etc.? By osmosis?

You'll begin to take on a myriad of roles such as secretary, surrogate parent, motivational speaker, accountant, cashier, nurse, psychologist, policeman, mediator, etc.

In addition to the daily routine of lesson planning and resource gathering, there are the frequent tasks of photocopying, replenishing classroom supplies, pumping air into deflated P.E. balls, hanging up student work or holiday decorations on the walls, correcting papers, collaborating with other teachers, attending staff meetings, etc.

I remember the day I started to submit my attendance report on my computer. It wouldn't connect to the server. I shut it down and turned it on several times. No luck. Finally, I asked the secretary for advice, and she suggested I put in a tech request for a nonworking computer.

Back in my classroom, I sat staring at the blank screen for several minutes wondering how to initiate a tech request with absolutely no ability to connect to the server. Suddenly, I had the archaic thought, *Pick up the phone and call the technology department for help.*

You'll need some system to stay on top of all that must be accomplished. What is your organizational fingerprint? Are you a list maker? Are you able to make and store mental notes? Do you rely completely on your smart phone?

**You're Thinking:** *If I don't get this deluge of work under control, I'm going to drown.*

**You Need to Tell Yourself:** *I need to prioritize my tasks. What needs to be done today, this week, this month? And just do it!*

## A Day in the Life

Due to the complexity of the job, you must be able to multi-task from the second you unlock your classroom door until your car pulls out of the parking lot. Take a look at a typical teaching day.

**7:55–8:25 a.m.** Arrive at school, turn on computers, check email, go to office to sign attendance report and payroll form, check staff room for snail mail, run thirty quick copies for math lesson, respond to an early morning text message from a parent. Run to the bathroom!

**8:25 a.m.** First bell rings. Pick up students from playground. Encounter two sets of parents waiting at the classroom door, each wanting to turn in money for student book orders. One needs change for a $10 bill. Students are settling in. Some children are standing at your desk waving permission slips and cash for the upcoming field trip.

**8:30 a.m.** Take attendance and lunch count. Phone rings twice with changes concerning today's dental screening in the library. Put students in ABC order for dental checkup. Go to the library. Return to class. Settle students down, remind them to put the new toothbrushes in their backpacks. Sure, you're not going to have a dental screening every week, but here's what will take its place: assemblies; hearing checks; head lice checks; fire, bus, and intruder alert drills; school picture day; etc.

**9:00 a.m.** Begin teaching math.

**10:00 a.m.** Recess bell rings. Keep Denise and Lloyd back for a five-minute "reteaching" on rounding numbers. Quickly check in homework. Call for substitute teacher for next week's professional-development workshop. Fill out a birthday certificate and pull a toy to celebrate Amber's birthday after recess. Run to the bathroom!

**10:15 a.m.** Teach language arts.

**11:30–12:15 p.m.** Lunch bell rings. Nourishment becomes secondary when you know you have forty-five minutes to set up equipment for P.E., check mailroom again for flyers going home, make personal phone calls, return books to the library, pick up the book order that came in, sign the group greeting card for a teacher's retirement party, fill up the pretzel jar for recess snacks (for younger grades), complete a union survey, and respond to parents' notes. Run to the bathroom!

**12:20–2:10 p.m.** End of day lessons.

**2:10 p.m.** Dismissal bell rings. More parents are waiting at the door. The phone is ringing. You feel the pressure of leaving your classroom quickly because it's your week for bus duty. If you're not at bus duty, you're quickly setting up for your afterschool tutoring session. Following this, you retrieve your fruit plate from the staff fridge to bring to the staff room for a teacher's baby shower at 3:00 p.m. Run to the bathroom!

**4:00 p.m.** You're back in the classroom making yourself a note: "Find glue gun—Friday's craft project."

Here are some *magic tricks* to help you succeed with organizing your classroom.

## Magic Trick #1: Straight Lines Make for a Smooth Start

One of my pet peeves is a mountain of backpacks piled up in front of my classroom door first thing in the morning. This is a problem you can easily avoid.

I trained my students the first day to drop off their backpacks side by side, against the outside classroom wall, in a straight line.

When we came in after the bell rang, the line formed naturally and the kids entered the classroom in an orderly fashion. There's no big rush to enter the class at the same time. It naturally spaces kids out. This little procedure takes minutes to teach, but it gave me a good feeling all year long to walk into my classroom without stumbling over backpacks. Everyone likes a smooth start to the day.

## Magic Trick #2: Pupils Pick up Piles of Papers, Pencils, & Paper Clips

"Wow," Mrs. Chow exclaimed, "How did they do that so fast?"

She was referring to my classroom magically transforming from disheveled to fastidious. The students were transitioning from making a Mother's Day craft to lining up for lunch.

The part she didn't hear was my command: "Johnny, floor inspection." Everyone understood it was time to pick up anything around their personal floor space. They knew they would be dismissed by the cleanest floor and the straightest rows. The net result was an instantly clean classroom.

It's all about expectations. Most kids feel more comfortable in an organized, tidy environment. Some of my students have no control over the chaos at home, but they are empowered when they realize they can keep their personal desk space clean and well-organized.

It also ensures a safe classroom for everyone, including yourself. I remember flying through the air like a trapeze artist when I tripped over a backpack left out in the aisle.

Just as teachers sit around after school talking about who has the most challenging student, custodians likewise chitchat about teachers with the messiest rooms.

The custodian will let you know how much he or she appreciates the clean floor. Sometimes that will translate into extra help when you need it. Remember this: there is no better friend to have on campus than the custodian.

## Magic Trick #3: A Dollop a Day Keeps the Doctor Away

Hoping to reduce the spread of illness in my classroom, I squeezed a dollop of hand sanitizer on students' hands as they lined up for lunch every day. With the threat of pandemic viruses, this procedure is more important than ever.

With twenty-four students in my classroom, hand washing with soap and water just wasn't practical. We had a designated time to be in the cafeteria.

Also, I relied on disinfectant wipes to clean students' desks . . . except the kids did the dirty work! They loved using the wipes to clean the desktops! Some of the more enthusiastic cleaners will wipe down their chairs, the inside of their desk, and everything else in sight. Be prepared to make this a quickie clean-up because the students will not want to quit.

By the end of your first year, you'll be adding your own personal magic tricks to the bag. Don't let yourself become overwhelmed. Soon these procedures will be done automatically. It just takes time, practice, patience, and experience to begin to feel comfortable about the many facets of the teaching profession.

**You're Thinking:** *Do I really want to be a teacher?*

**You Need to Tell Yourself:** *Have faith. Take it one step at a time. Every day will become easier. My friends tell me, "Procedures become automatic. You'll be amazed by the end of the first month how efficient you've become!"*

## CHAPTER 3

# Time Management

*In order that people may be happy in their work, these three things are needed: they must be fit for it, they must not do too much of it, and they must have a sense of success in it.*

—JOHN RUSKIN

Teaching is just the tip of the iceberg. Extra duties that may come with your job are planning field trips, decorating classroom bulletin boards, preparing craft projects, telephoning parents, putting on classroom parties, coaching a sport, helping with the Parent Teacher Club or School Site Council, attending union meetings, attending or facilitating professional-development workshops, being active on school committees, participating in school clubs, tutoring after school, and so forth.

As you can see, the notion of merely teaching—and only teaching—may have gone the way of the little schoolhouse on the prairie. You will be asked to shoulder many additional duties and responsibilities beyond the classroom. In fact, your principal may have noticed your extra talents on the resume you turned in. Athletic skills, yearbook experience, or an art background could influence him or her to grab you from the group of job candidates.

My friend believes that she was hired due to the fact that she played soccer in high school. She was enlisted to be the soccer coach for the first five years of her career.

## The Temptation to Overachieve

You'll want to please people but not at the cost of encroaching on your personal life or flirting with teacher burnout. You must quickly figure out how to sustain your energy and enthusiasm for the long haul to make this your career.

Listen and learn from the mistakes these new teachers made so that you don't fall prey to the same pitfalls.

Lisa was a competent, young kindergarten teacher of great promise. However, her high achieving Type A personality was her undoing. She was highly competitive, work obsessed, and meticulous to the extreme.

While other teachers put in a long day and turned the key to their classrooms at around 4:30 p.m., she was just picking up steam. When other teachers were home with their families, Lisa was still in her classroom putting up impeccable bulletin boards at 7:00 p.m.

It wasn't unusual for the night custodian to reveal Lisa's nocturnal habits during his early morning coffee conversations. Bear in mind that, as a teacher, your proclivities are not private. You will be watched, whether it's by parents, custodians, administrators, colleagues, etc. (There's a case to be made for not going out in public without a shave or full make-up—at the very least, comb your hair!)

Lisa was such a perfectionist that, for example, rather than trust her kindergarteners to cut out butterfly shapes for her science lesson, she'd spend hours cutting them out herself in order to garnish praise from the parents as they admired the finished product.

You couldn't walk into Lisa's room without letting out a sigh of admiration. It was touted by the district as the quintessential classroom, and it became a showcase and a destination point for new kindergarten teachers to behold. She was becoming something of a star, so it was nearly impossible for Lisa to decline the superintendent's offer to serve on the Leadership Committee.

Likewise, her administrator thought she'd be a natural for heading up the after-school Art Club. While she enjoyed this extracurricular activity, it was quite a burden for her to find the time she needed to complete the course work for the master's degree program she was simultaneously pursuing.

Everyone was amazed at how much she was accomplishing. Her perfectly coifed hair and sophisticated attire belied the frenetic pace it took to keep all of her irons in the fire.

There is an old saying that goes like this: "If you want something done well, ask a busy person to do it." She was the go-to girl for any little task the principal needed doing. Like Ado Annie, from the musical *Oklahoma*, she was just a girl who couldn't say no.

Luckily, my first administrator had a different philosophy. He told me, "As a new teacher, I don't want to see you volunteering for anything during your first two years."

He was perceptive and nurturing, and, looking back, I appreciate his advice even more now than I did at that time.

If Lisa had had him for an administrator, she may have stayed in the profession for more than a paltry three years. She crashed and burned!

Those who knew her best recalled her confession, "I just couldn't face another year of being pulled in so many directions."

She went on to become a real estate agent. Sadly, the classroom lost a talented teacher who may have survived had she been able to prioritize and balance her activities more effectively.

## Penny Wise And Pound Foolish

So many young, cash-poor teachers are faced with the great temptation to say yes to any activity that carries a stipend. The activities can range from sitting on a committee to coaching a sport.

The allure of these kinds of monetary rewards made a good friend of mine, Allie, enslaved to a multitude of extra duties. She was supporting a disabled family member. Her brother and his small family came to rely on her, not only for a roof overhead but also for the supplemental financial support that she provided.

During any typical school year, you could be sure to see Allie agreeing to take on any after-school activity that offered a stipend, whether it be after-school tutoring, coaching a sport, or taking on the role of union representative. She knew she was overtaxing her time and leading a stressful life, yet the stipends filled the gap between her family's needs and a beginning teacher's sparse salary. She realized she was saying yes to assignments that she really didn't have time for.

## Say No in a Nice Way; Say Yes to Having More Time!

Allie's situation is not unique. Kenny was a young man who had the responsibility of a wife and two-year-old twins.

He was a brand-new teacher who was trying to make a name for himself by volunteering to do anything that was offered. He simply couldn't say no to after-school math tutoring, coaching basketball and softball, and organizing and purchasing P.E. equipment for the whole school.

Ironically, he was so overwhelmed by the acquired responsibilities that he became disillusioned and disgruntled with teachers, staff, and students for not cooperating with him. He took on the persona of the martyr who was doing more than his fair share at the school.

The following year, Kenny had the opportunity to transfer to another school, even though it meant trading his preferred grade level (fifth) for a hectic kindergarten assignment. Who knows if the tradeoff was worth it?

**You're Thinking:** *I really want to be noticed. I can show my administrator that I'm a team player by volunteering to be on the Site Council.*

**You Need to Tell Yourself:** *The best way to impress my administrator is getting my kids fired up about learning and building positive relationships.*

Frequently you may find yourself being asked to team up with a colleague or colleagues to perform extra activities. Let me illustrate my lesson of "hard knocks" where, had I employed the skill of saying no nicely, I would have saved myself considerable angst.

I said yes to Betty, a colleague who I believed genuinely needed my assistance with an important school program about drug awareness and prevention. Our school's program, similar to many others across the nation, targeted early adolescents in educating them about the dangers of illicit substances.

Betty approached me one afternoon and said, "I need a partner to head up the anti-drug campaign. There's a stipend attached."

"Sure, I'll help with that," I cheerfully replied.

We set about splitting up the attendant tasks equally: preparing a budget, ordering T-shirts, planning a field trip, securing the bus, dispensing ribbons for the entire school body, and organizing an end-of-the-week rally.

Feeling satisfied with my completion of the budget, arranging the field trip, and the ordering of the ribbons, I walked down to Betty's room to inform her of my progress.

When I asked how her tasks were coming along, she snapped defensively, "I've just been so swamped. I haven't had time to think about it! This grant-writing project is taking up way more time than I thought it would. And I'm rethinking my plans to get my master's degree. The yearbook project definitely was not a good thing to take on while I'm planning for my daughter's wedding."

She rolled her eyes and sighed when I reminded her about the upcoming field trip next week. The middle grade students would be traveling to the local convention center to hear speakers donned in their brand-new "Don't Fall for Drugs" T-shirts. I was flabbergasted to find out the bus request and the T-shirt order had not yet been submitted!

I left her room feeling angry and disillusioned, and I stuffed my inclination to hurl one of my favorite quotes at her: "Your lack of planning does not my emergency make."

However, I allowed it to become just that.

Aside from my frustrations, I knew how disappointed our students would be if our school would be the only one not attending the assembly.

I immediately telephoned the T-shirt company and shamelessly begged for their assistance in rushing a big order of one hundred T-shirts. Then I phoned the district bus coordinator and secured the bus for the big day.

The event went off as planned and was a big success. Betty and I both received our stipend, and I learned to be realistic about the time commitments I was so casually committing to.

You don't want to put yourself on the precipice like the aforementioned teachers. Start each school year with measured steps. Take an honest inventory of your goals, responsibilities, and priorities. Carefully develop time-management skills. Write down what your priorities are, taking into consideration time for family, friends, work, community, church service, etc. Divide your time accordingly. Realize that too much time devoted to any one of these areas may be robbing time from other important facets of your life.

Overcommitting yourself to good causes can have a negative effect. You may get so stressed out that you become crabby, exhausted, or even ill.

When colleagues come calling, be honest. It never pays to entangle yourself in phantom excuses. Trying to keep your stories straight is an energy zapper in itself. Be gracious and let them know how much you value their activity or cause. Tell them that you would genuinely like to help at a time when your life isn't so busy.

Remember, time management is all about being aware of what you're obligated to do and how much time you *realistically* have to accomplish certain tasks.

For example, you *must* contact parents for academic awards assemblies, but you're not obligated to phone parents on a weekly basis. You *must* have a wall decorated with student work before the Open House program at your school, but you're not obligated to turn your room into a jungle with papier-mâché trees in every corner. You *must* have your report cards completed and ready for parent-teacher conference week, but you're not obligated to have every single piece of paper for the trimester graded and notated before the meeting.

It's true that your beginning salary is notoriously lean, and the temptation to supplement with stipends can be practically irresistible. Honor yourself as a new teacher: know your limitations and fortify yourself against the pressures of accepting too many jobs. Be realistic in what commitments you make. Weigh all the pros and cons before you say yes.

**You're Thinking:** *My baby needs new clothes. I should take on that coaching position.*

**You Need to Tell Yourself:** *If I take the coaching position, my baby will be well dressed, but I'll miss playtime with her for two solid months.*

CLUBS
TUTORING
COACHING
COMMITTEES
UNION
TEACHING
FAMILY & FRIENDS
JUGGLING ONE TOO MANY?
¢2

## CHAPTER 4

# Classroom Management: It's Monumental!

*Classroom management is like the white screen in a movie theater. We always ignore it, but without it, the show can't go on.*

—Rick Smith

It may be that your classroom decor is captivating enough to be featured on the cover of *Scholastic Teacher* magazine, your lessons are impeccable, and you feel confident about the curriculum you plan to teach. All of this is for naught unless you have good behavior-management skills.

A number of books have addressed this topic, and you will be able to pull a little from this one and pick up a tip from that one. But what really counts is your ability to create an atmosphere that promotes learning and adopt a discipline strategy that *you* believe in.

> Students Thrive on Structure
> and Well-Defined Expectations.

Students will respond positively when given clear guidelines for behavior. Teachers with a good management style and an orderly atmosphere in their classroom often develop a reputation for being a "favorite teacher" at the school.

The foundation of a well-managed classroom is a positive relationship with your students coupled with high expectations. Social relationships are based on a mutual understanding of trust and respect.

## Modeling

Mrs. Stone dropped into my classroom one afternoon anxious to share a success story. She was the resource teacher who taught a small remediation group of which Anna was a part.

"I think I got through to Anna," she said. "You know how sick I am of explaining over and over again how to enter my classroom without disrupting the others? Anna's barreling through my door every day is driving me crazy!

"Today was different! I had her sit down and watch two different styles of entering my room. First, I recreated her boisterous entry. Then, I modeled my expectations. I opened the door quietly, took my seat at the table, made eye contact with Anna (who played the role of the teacher), and waited for directions.

"I asked Anna, 'Which way do you think works best in this room?' She quickly acknowledged that the second choice was best. No further words were spoken and the problem with Anna was resolved."

Modeling positive behavior will help students better understand their responsibilities in the classroom.

Sam Stevens successfully taught fourth grade for about six years when he had to take a three-month leave of absence due to personal health problems. He thought he had arranged for a dependable, effective long-term substitute to fill his shoes. The sub followed his curriculum to a T, gave the trimester assessments, and fulfilled every schoolwide protocol for providing instruction.

Yet when Mr. Stevens returned from his leave of absence, almost everybody on campus made subtle and sometimes blatant comments on how glad they were to see him and how relieved they were to say goodbye to the sub. In spite of her meticulous lesson planning and presentation, there was one area in which her skills were lacking—classroom management.

> Remain Consistent in All You Say and Do.
> Give Students a Clear Picture of What Is Nonnegotiable.

"When I returned in December," Mr. Stevens recalled, "I walked into a classroom where nobody listened to a word I said. Rules were clearly posted, yet none were followed. I realized that I would have to start over, as if it were September. It took me longer to teach my rules, procedures, and routines at that point in the year since many of my students had already established negative behaviors and habits that were hard to break."

## Procedures, Transitions, and Routines

First of all, it is important that you distinguish the difference between classroom procedures and your discipline plan. Procedures do not carry consequences. They require students to do a simple task a certain way every time. Some good examples are start-of-the-day tasks, quieting down quickly, lining up for recess, fire-drill practice, library visits, putting chairs up at the end of the day, transitioning to another classroom for instruction, changing activities within the classroom, restroom breaks, sharpening a broken pencil, etc.

So now you're asking, "How do I teach my students the correct procedure for sharpening pencils?"

It sounds pretty silly, but effective teachers will cover the most mundane tasks and teach the students the correct procedure to accomplish each one. It will eliminate wasted time later when you have to stop and explain the procedure right in the middle of your lesson.

You will find that the time invested in explicitly teaching procedures (and practicing them) during the first weeks of school pays dividends all year long. It sounds so simple; however, it is often overlooked. The benefits of teaching students the proper procedures are lasting.

What about those precious moments between lessons or right after recess and lunch? That's when you want your class to run like a well-oiled machine. It can be done.

You will want to clearly state, model, demonstrate, rehearse, and practice classroom transitions at length. This is especially true with the younger grades. Having your students act out the routine is fun and effective. Many love the dramatization of it all. It is essential that you do this during the first few weeks of school. Even though you're anxious to present your treasure trove of lessons, you will make a wise investment by putting a lot of time in rehearsing and modeling procedures at the start of the year. Once your students are certain as to what their responsibilities are, then the procedures become a habit or a routine. They'll do it automatically, like flicking on a light switch, without any prompting from you.

Still, it's always a good idea to review the routines throughout the year and praise students when you notice them following your plans. You may have the most orderly line of students walking down the hallway in September, but they might not even remember what the procedure was by the middle of November.

I found that an ideal time to review classroom rules and routines is when a new student enrolled in my class. The other students modeled the expected behaviors.

I remember getting off the school bus from a swimming field trip in the late spring. Two classes were on the bus, mine and Mr. Steele's. I waited patiently for my students to line up as they departed the bus. Mr. Steele's students ran helter-skelter off the bus toward their classroom. He was way ahead of the line and not looking back. The bus driver looked out of the bus at me and asked, "Do you know that Casey is still on the bus? He won't get off, and he doesn't have his shoes or socks on!"

Casey was Mr. Steele's first-grade student, notorious for causing problems on campus. I got back on the bus, found his shoes and socks, and helped him put them on. He walked back to class with us, whereupon I delivered him to Mr. Steele, who didn't even notice that he was missing from class! This was a classroom with ill-defined procedures.

## Attention-Getters

When you are ready to give detailed instructions and you don't want to repeat yourself endlessly, try the following attention-getters: oral cues, hand clapping, hand signals, sound cues, etc. You will have to decide which ones are appropriate for your students' age.

There will be many situations where students need to give you their complete attention at once. This is especially true on field trips or at assemblies.

Here are a couple of good examples of callbacks (oral cues):

Teacher: "One, two."

Students: "Eyes on you."

Teacher: "Class, class."

Students: "Yes, yes."

Train students explicitly that the cue will be given again if all eyes are not immediately on you. With practice they become quite adept at responding and giving you their full attention.

This is a great strategy to have in your toolkit because it's transferable to *any* person in authority. I've had parents, aides, and docents express their appreciation for empowering them in this way.

For example, it used to bother me when, on a field trip, docents were disseminating fascinating information while only about one-third of my class listened. Let's face it, there are so many things to see, it's hard to keep kids focused. Before every field trip, we reviewed the docent's role and proper etiquette. They knew that if they kept their eyes on the docent while he/she was speaking, they would be guaranteed an opportunity to look around afterward at all the *cool* things.

Here are a few others you may want to try. Clap a pattern, and students repeat the pattern back:

Teacher: clap, clap, (pause) clap

Students: clap, clap, (pause) clap

Another example is to combine words with clapping:

"If you can hear me, clap once."

Some students clap.

Then say, "If you can hear me, clap twice."

By now, all students are attentive and clap twice.

Some teachers begin teaching before corralling the group's attention. Often the volume of the teacher's voice increases so as to be heard over the students' chatter.

The result is chaos . . . and I am humbly speaking from experience here.

My first year of teaching, I had a challenging class of thirty-two fourth graders. I noticed myself talking louder and louder to be heard above the din. My class really made a turnaround when I began using some of these attention-getting strategies.

Sometimes it is appropriate to simply stop teaching and just be *quiet*. It's one of most **effective** attention-getters. Generally, kids stop talking and turn their attention to the teacher.

Something as simple as turning off the classroom lights can refocus their attention and get kids back on track.

With older kids, these techniques may or may not be useful; however, I know a middle school teacher who uses a train whistle to transition to a new classroom activity or anytime she needs their full attention. The wooden train whistle has a very pleasant, soothing sound.

But, for the very young, there is a trick that I have used that is magical. These two words—"pin drop"—alert my students that I expect complete silence. Sometimes all I needed to do was pretend to drop a pin with a hand gesture. I was always amazed at how well it worked, especially with kindergarten students. A fourth-grade teacher uses the same words when her phone rings and, immediately, the students are silent.

There are numerous attention-getters. Make up your own or find them online.

## Reinforce Positive Behaviors

*If you must raise your voice, do it to cheer someone on.*

—ANONYMOUS

In their book *The First Days of School*, Harry and Rosemary Wong give splendid advice on establishing procedures. They present detailed guidelines for teaching students everything from how to pass papers correctly across the rows to starting up your day with a morning routine.

The Wongs also give excellent examples on how to reinforce positive behaviors through the use of praise and encouragement.

They draw the distinction between *nice* praise versus *effective* praise.[1]

For example, I may tell a student, "Roy, you're such a smart young man." However, it's going to have a stronger impact if I say, "Roy, you aced your times sevens test! I know you put in that extra time to memorize your facts this week."

Words of praise are powerful. Nevertheless, try to be specific about what the student did well.

## Tangible versus Intangible Rewards

Your school may have tangible rewards to pass out to your students at your discretion. You may see everything from "caught ya being good" tickets to postcards printed with a teacher checklist of positive behaviors. Parents are always thrilled to receive good news from school.

Some teachers have treasure chests with inexpensive prizes for motivating and/or rewarding students. Older students will appreciate extra recess time or free homework passes. No matter what you give them, your students will respond to tangible rewards. Intangible rewards consist mainly of kind words or gestures such as a silent round of applause, a high five, a thumbs up, pats on the back, etc. No matter which you use, acknowledge positive behavior at every opportunity. Sometimes it's wise to have a class discussion reflecting on how well students are conducting themselves. For example: "I'm so pleased that you guys remembered where to put your library books without being told. Tell me how you did that."

Not only is reinforcing good behavior effective, but it also makes you *aware of the positive things* that are happening in your class. It's way too easy to get fixated on the negatives.

## It's a Given: Problems *Will* Occur in Your Classroom

Conflict is a natural part of growing up. Students make mistakes. When minor or major problems arise, you must maintain your self-control and stay calm. Never involve yourself in a power struggle with your students. Don't yell, scream, or throw things, as some teachers (who have lost their cool) have done. I have even heard of substitute teachers walking off the job in the midst of an uncontrollable group of students!

My best friend's son, Calvin, a second grader, came home in tears.

"I hate my teacher!" he told his mom, "She's mean!"

He went on to explain how the students are always misbehaving.

"Mom, our teacher yells at us. Today she threw Gracie's backpack across the room!"

The next day, Calvin related a story about the teacher flinging a book and a pencil across the room. Consequently, Calvin's mom transferred him to another school. Other parents pulled their kids out as well! There should never be a moment when a teacher loses his/her composure.

> Remember That Conflict Is Inevitable
> While Combat Is Optional.

Things aren't always going to run smoothly in your classroom. When you start feeling stress, take some deep breaths and speak in softer tones.

I learned a little secret from a thirty-year veteran teacher. She never says, "Shh-shh-shh, shh-shh-shh" to quiet students. Instead, she quietly says, "I need the class to be quiet before we can go onto our next lesson."

I've adopted this strategy. The kids will usually ignore your "Shh-shh-shh" anyway! However, the class will respond when you change the tone of your voice and simply speak lower. You'll get their attention and keep your sanity.

Keep in mind that teachers are autonomous in creating a classroom atmosphere. Your attitude is like an ignition key to a student's motor. You can either turn them on or turn them off.

For example, Jeremy's art teacher, Mrs. Monroe, asked him several times to put away his colored pencils. He ignored her. Moving closer to him, she used her loudest voice, saying, "Didn't I tell you to put those pencils away at least three times?"

Jeremy was a student who needed lots of personal space. He lashed out and used both hands to push her away from himself. This butting of heads led to Jeremy's expulsion from school. Mrs. Monroe was so inflexible that it triggered an impulsive, negative reaction from Jeremy.

Six months later he returned and was placed in my third- grade class. My goal was to establish a good relationship with him from the start. He was a very sensitive boy and couldn't handle pressure from adults or peers.

One peculiarity of his was his fear of other classmates touching his desk. I arranged his desk so others couldn't bother him. I wanted him to feel safe.

When presenting my lessons, I knew he'd perform if I didn't turn the pressure gauge up too high.

For example, he wouldn't write a three-paragraph report, but I could coax him to produce one nicely written paragraph. It was a great compromise. The following year, I'd see him on campus and receive that sweet, shy smile.

Another teacher, Mr. Gutierrez, heard horror stories about a boy named Dallas. He had a reputation of running away from school and throwing temper tantrums. The school psychologist said he was the most dysfunctional student she had ever worked with. When Mr. Gutierrez saw Dallas was on his fifth-grade class roster, he was apprehensive.

"I didn't know what to expect," Mr. Gutierrez remembered. "It didn't take me long to realize that Dallas was a brilliant student. I nicknamed him 'Mr. Vocabulary' and gave him the positive recognition he was crying out for by calling him to answer a question correctly at every opportunity.

"Early on I realized that Dallas didn't like being seated near other students. He became very agitated when doing group work. I moved his seat to the very back of the class, away from other students. He could function fine when he was provided plenty of personal space and lots of positive feedback. Dallas had a great year, and the counselor and other teachers couldn't believe the changes they saw in him."

## Love And Logic: A Sensible Program!

One of the more powerful and well-known behavior-management programs is Love and Logic, developed by Jim Fay and Foster W. Cline. Jim Fay is one of America's most sought-after presenters in the fields of parenting and positive discipline. He has written numerous books on the subject. Cofounder of the Love and Logic Institute, Foster W. Cline, MD, also coauthored books with Jim Fay on this topic.

The two rules of Love and Logic are "First, take good care of yourself by setting limits without anger, lectures, threats, or repeated warnings. Second, when a child causes a problem, hand it back in a caring way."[2]

Natural consequences, employed with empathy and dignity rather than with cruelty and ridicule, extinguish negative behavior.

A teacher equipped with Love and Logic skills may whisper, smile, and use a gentle voice when presenting logical consequences. They even conclude with a pleasant "thank you!" They give students choices. In turn, students feel in control and become problem solvers.

Here are examples of the ineffective technique versus the Love and Logic technique.

*Ineffective Technique*
"Don't talk to me in that tone of voice!"

*Love and Logic Technique*
"I'll listen as soon as your voice is as calm as mine."

*Ineffective Technique*
"Don't be late for class."

*Love and Logic Technique*
"All those who arrive on time go home on time."

*Ineffective Technique*
"Don't try to turn in sloppy papers to me."

*Love and Logic Technique*
"I'll be glad to accept all papers that meet the neatness standard for this room."

*Ineffective Technique*
"Turn in your assignment on time or you'll get a lower grade."

*Love and Logic Technique*
"I give full credit for papers turned in on time."

If you are unfamiliar with the Love and Logic program, it would be worth your time to put it on your reading list.

## Positive Discipline: Problem-Solving Skills

You can avoid a lot of tattling, whining, and complaining by teaching your students to become problem solvers. One of the best books for running a smooth classroom is *Positive Discipline in the Classroom* by Jane Nelsen, Lynn Lott, and Judy Arleen Glenn.

These authors describe how class meetings, effective communication skills, and teachers helping other teachers can bring order and civility into any classroom.

They state in their book, "When children feel safe—that they belong and are significant—they thrive. They learn, they develop into capable people, and they develop social interests. When children believe they do not belong and are not significant, they adopt survival (defensive) behavior."[3]

Minor problems typically occur during recess. Students return to class anxious to tattle on another student or express hurt feelings. This is a transitional time and other kids are settling down.

With minor problems, I teach my students to use the "I Message." It puts the responsibility on the students.

This technique invests a lot of time front-loading the correct way for each party to respond. It takes a lot of role-playing and practice to teach students the respectful manner of problem solving and apologizing. However, it is all worth it because it practically eliminates the problem of tattletaling.

For example, a student pushes ahead of another and cuts in line. The offended party makes eye contact with the offender and states, "I don't like it when you push me and take cuts in line." The other student makes eye contact (very important) and apologizes. The one who has been wronged says, "I accept your apology."

Here is another example of how the "I Message" works. A student might say, "I feel bad when you won't share the soccer ball, and I wish you would share." They talk it out and resolve the problem.

Keep in mind that you will have to make a judgment call on when the "I Message" addresses the negative behavior. It works well when there's a situation like poking and pinching in line. Of course, a fight that breaks out at recess will be handled much differently. But wherever possible, teach your students to become problem solvers.

## A Program That Works: Capturing Kids' Hearts

My school district adopted the Capturing Kids' Hearts Process, which I found to be helpful with my classroom management. Capturing Kids' Hearts (CKH) is powered by The Flippen Group®, one of North America's largest educator training companies and fastest-growing leadership development organizations. On any given school day, the Capturing Kids' Hearts Process and curricula positively impact millions of students in districts nationwide.

The heart of the Capturing Kids' Hearts Process includes specific actions teachers take to make the students feel safe and connected.

For example, teachers greet students at the door in the morning with a fist bump or a handshake, and they end the day with a meaningful message.

In addition, I relied on my classroom Social Contract developed by my students at the start of every school year. We brainstormed what behaviors we commit to, and I made a poster of these expectations, which each student signed to demonstrate their commitment and accountability. Then I displayed it on the wall. The Capturing Kids' Hearts Process provides classroom-management tools, including a relational approach to handling misbehavior.

There are so many programs to help you develop your classroom-management style. The aforementioned approaches and processes are what worked for me. Find one that you feel comfortable using, and remember, be consistent. Consistency is the keystone to any effective management program.

## CHAPTER 5

# Who's in the Class?

*The marvelous richness of human experience would lose something of rewarding joy if there were no limitations to overcome. The hilltop hour would not be half so wonderful if there were no dark valleys to traverse.*

—Helen Keller

You probably have an idealistic vision of the types of personalities you'll find behind those smiling faces. Some students fit the norm of the active, happy, healthy child. Yet a certain percentage of the kids in the classroom will have special needs, everything from personality or mood disorders to learning disabilities.

> Special-Needs Students
> Need Special Understanding!

Traditionally, children with severe handicaps were kept in special classes. In today's climate of mainstreaming, the chances are you may be responsible for the education of students who are oppositional defiant, bipolar, autistic, hyperactive, have attention deficit, etc. I have seen kids with these problems in my classroom, and you are likely to as well.

## Home Environment and How It Affects Learning

I was asked this question in my job interview: "How much do you want to know about your students?" The correct answer? *Everything!*

Let me tell you why you **must** make it your mission to be aware of the personal life of each individual in your class.

I'll never forget teaching, reteaching, and reviewing the principles of writing a good summary. Most of the class was catching on, with the exception of poor little Riley. As I pulled her aside to work with her individually, she revealed the reason for her inability to focus.

"Teacher," Riley confided, "I couldn't sleep last night because I kept seeing the picture in my head of my dad holding an axe attacking my uncle."

I verified later that dad was indeed arrested for such a heinous act. The uncle was severely injured, but he survived.

I felt as though I had to recalibrate my teaching priorities for this dear child. Writing a good summary would have to take a back seat to making her feel safe at school and, to the extent possible, at home as well.

School has to become a safety net for those children where life at home is dysfunctional. This was no isolated incident with Riley. Over the course of the next three years, I encountered other fragile souls. For example, Michele witnessed Dad, fresh out of jail, hold a gun to Mom's head. Then there was Jeffrey. He witnessed his mom's suicide.

The term you will hear about these traumatic events that students experience is referred to as ACEs (Adverse Childhood

Experiences). These can include violence, physical and/or emotional abuse, mental health issues, or substance abuse problems. Toxic stress from ACEs can change brain development and affect how the body responds to stress. ACEs are linked to chronic health problems, addictions, and mental illness in adulthood.[1]

There are also serious ramifications for kids whose problems stem more from neglect than abuse. It's not unusual for kids to go home to an empty house after school. Because of the economic demands on American families, many two-parent or single-parent families must work full time. These children, by necessity, must become more autonomous at an early age.

For the most part, self-care kids are surviving, and responsible parents are monitoring their well-being. However, there are those families who don't have the resources to pull this off.

Children left alone may experience fear and loneliness or take on a heightened sense of responsibility. My colleague, Lori, told an unforgettable story about one of her third graders.

"Gabe was a latchkey kid," Lori recalled. "He was the oldest child with two younger sisters. One day for sharing time, he told the story of how he foraged for dinner. Mom had left him in charge. He went to the cupboard, as was his habit when Mom worked beyond the dinner hour. Only this time the cupboard was bare! When his sisters' whines turned to wails because of their hunger pangs, Gabe went knocking on the neighbors' doors. He triumphantly returned with enough bread and peanut butter to feed his little family."

Young kids are left home alone for all kinds of reasons and the uncoached ones are not afraid to tell why. I've heard tales such as, "My dad was at the casino gambling" or "My parents were out of town for the weekend." These unsupervised children are forced to learn self-sufficiency early in life.

## Restrictions and Regulations

Balance your natural inclination to rescue students with a firm knowledge of the limits placed upon you by your district's legal restrictions and regulations.

This is a lesson I learned several years ago.

My schedule was such that I arrived at school extremely early. As I pulled into the parking lot, it was not uncommon to find Timothy shivering in the rain, sitting on the curb at 6:30 a.m.

His hardworking single mother had to be at work early, so he huddled near my parking area on those days when Grandma or Grandpa couldn't take him to school. Naturally, I invited Timothy into the sheltered comfort of my classroom where he stayed until the school cafeteria opened at 7:30 a.m.

My administrator must have noticed this little scenario because I soon found myself in her office discussing Timothy's circumstances.

She nodded and explained sympathetically, "It is the district's policy that children cannot come to school before supervision is provided. That means you need to call Timothy's mom and explain that he cannot be on the premises before 7:30 a.m."

I knew my administrator to have almost limitless compassion for her students. Therefore, I didn't try to champion the cause for Timothy. I realized that her attention to the liability issue was for my protection as well as the student's.

## Children with Special Needs

As you have seen, students face traumas, neglect, and other psychological and sociological pressures that may require a little TLC from you. This is certainly true of students with other conditions, disorders, or learning disabilities.

As a new teacher, you're going to hear these terms flying at you: ADD (attention deficit disorder), ADHD (attention deficit hyperactivity disorder), autism, special-needs students, etc.

## Autism

Autism is becoming more prevalent, and it's very likely you'll encounter an autistic student in your class. Extensive research is currently being done on autism; however, the causes remain unclear. Autism Spectrum Disorder (ASD) defines the irregular behaviors on a continuum from mild to severe. These include communication deficits such as responding inappropriately in conversations, misreading nonverbal interactions, or having difficulty building friendships appropriate to their age. In addition, people with ASD may be overly dependent on routines.[2]

You may have an autistic child in your class and not even know it. They may not yet have been diagnosed. Try to recognize the symptoms as early as possible. Be ready to reach out to your school counselor, resource teacher, or administrator for support.

Be aware of these common symptoms: compulsive behaviors, lack of emotion, trouble tolerating noises or being touched, and looking at the mouth of the person speaking instead of making eye contact.

These children may even exhibit extreme behaviors such as spinning, head banging, biting, scratching, or endlessly repeating phrases. Many have trouble making transitions and are rigidly dependent on schedules.

I had a third grader, Aiden, who was diagnosed as autistic. He had a personal aide in the classroom. Aiden had low social skills but was very intelligent. He read well and could retain most of what he read. However, at recess, he was a loner, wandering along the periphery of the playground all by himself.

I had taken great pains to accommodate Aiden. I had him sitting near the front where he could see the daily class schedule at a glance.

On one occasion, I changed the schedule due to an afternoon assembly. When he realized this, it sent him into a tailspin. He became highly agitated and started banging his head on the desk, shouting, "Why aren't we doing silent reading?"

His personal aide came to the rescue and took him out of the class where he could regain his composure. This incident made me realize the importance of giving Aiden a "heads up" whenever the schedule changed.

Autistic children are typically hypersensitive to visual and auditory stimulation; therefore, it is critical that the classroom be peaceful and well ordered.

## ADD & ADHD

Some people subscribe to the notion that kids are overly medicated for the convenience of parents and teachers. It wasn't until I had firsthand experience teaching children who had ADD and ADHD that I became more sophisticated in my thinking. I realized the question of whether or not to medicate is complex, and there are many factors to be considered. However, it's undeniable that there are some medications that truly do improve the social and academic school experience for these kids.

The year I taught fourth grade, I noticed Gary's inability to stay focused. He was constantly fidgeting, playing in his desk, distracting his neighbors, making strange noises, chewing his erasers, and leaving his seat without permission.

After exhausting every behavior-management technique I knew, I realized that Gary's actions were not within the realm of his control. (Be aware that it's never appropriate for you to suggest to parents that they medicate their child.)

I was relieved when one of the members of the student study team, a team comprised of the teacher, the administrator, the school psychologist, the resource teacher, and others, suggested to Gary's parents they take him to their physician for a complete evaluation. I was only too happy to fill in the lengthy questionnaire required by the doctor. Most doctors request teacher input before prescribing medications.

The change in Gary was *dramatic* once the correct dosage of medications was established! All the nervous, impulsive behaviors vanished. His demeanor was calm. He applied himself. His self-esteem grew right along with his academic skills.

When I saw the same scenario work with Conner and Jack, I knew I could not arbitrarily dismiss medications as a valuable resource. These experiences made me a believer!

On the other hand, there are children who may *appear* to have ADD or ADHD.

For example, Pete's previous years' teachers kept coming to me and asking, "How's Pete doing? He's so ADHD. Is he on meds yet?"

I was baffled. Pete was physical, yes, but impulsively so, no. He was very immature and could easily take over my classroom if I let him. He responded well to the rules and expectations I had for my classroom. He just needed the "teacher *look*" to be reminded of acceptable classroom behavior.

Later, I learned from Pete's mother that his previous two years in school were devoid of that structure. It was clear to me that Pete needed close monitoring, not medications.

**You're Thinking:** *This child needs medication!*

**You Need to Tell Yourself:** *It's time to make a referral to the school psychologist.*

## Pilfering: A Perennial Problem

As a teacher, your natural inclination is to trust every child that enters your classroom. It took me four years of disillusionment to finally realize that field-trip money, purses and wallets, and special crafts supplies have to be placed in a locked cabinet.

Every year I have had one or more incidents in which students have stolen from me or from their peers. The most infamous pilferer was nine-year-old Andrew.

That year, I was at a loss to explain the mysterious disappearances of a case of soda (one can at a time), several pairs of special crafts scissors, distinctive pens and pencils, and cash collected for a class field trip.

The mystery was solved a couple of months later when our fourth-grade class toured the historic Sutter's Fort in Sacramento, California.

At the Old Time Print Shop, a docent demonstrated his craft. Part of the printing process included the use of various sized brass letters, ranging from one inch to four inches in height. Letters and numbers were everywhere . . . on tables, on shelves, and buried in sawdust shavings on the old wooden floor.

The glint of the gold letters caught Andrew's eye. Later, on our bus ride home, Andrew started giving away brass letters to his friends.

The next day, several kids tattled on him. Faced with the hard evidence, Andrew not only admitted to the petty larceny on the field trip but he also fessed up to being the culprit behind my missing classroom items.

Small locks on a cabinet in your room will give you peace of mind and prevent opportunistic moments for theft. Keep cash, personal belongings, and other precious items locked up and out of sight.

**You're Thinking:** *My purse will be fine right here in my drawer.*

**You Need to Tell Yourself:** *I shouldn't tempt sticky-fingered students.*

## Create Your Own Culture

Most educators are aware of the influence of the media on preteens and teens. Advertising and marketing to a young, impressionable audience is extremely profitable!

With social media comes the hyperawareness of sexuality, even among very young children. It has seeped deeply into the elementary grades.

Coming in as a new teacher, I knew I would see the innocent boy-girl attractions, but what I didn't expect was the proliferation of explicit sexual comments and conversations.

I had a kindergarten student tell a girl that he was going to sleep with her as soon as he was eighteen.

I recently heard on the local news that an eighth-grade girl was having sex with boys in the girls bathroom.

You, as the teacher, especially at the elementary level, need to be vigilant and aware, addressing these issues when necessary and bringing it up to your administrator if warranted.

Most importantly, you will want to create a culture in your classroom that reflects your values and what makes you feel comfortable.

For me, personally, I created a culture in my classroom that supported my philosophy of "You have a right to be a kid." We had many conversations about what is and what is not appropriate. Most children felt a sense of safety in this atmosphere.

## Watch for Red Flags!

If you see a student exhibiting unusual sexual behavior, be watchful. I was way too naive by overlooking some of Antonia's peculiar behaviors the year I taught fourth grade.

She, "Tony," was overly flirtatious with the boys and dressed provocatively.

If she wasn't being sent to the office for her dress-code violations, then it was for inappropriate sexual comments made to other students.

I rationalized this as the combined influence of older teenage sisters and too much screen time. Nothing could have prepared me for the real truth.

I was flabbergasted when I read the headlines in the news: "Local couple arrested in connection with suspicion of sexually abusing their four daughters, ages nine through seventeen."

Tony's parents were arrested for child molestation of Tony and her three sisters, Bobby, Frankie, and Charlie. The maternal grandmother turned them in after the oldest child told her of years of sexual abuse at the hands of their own mother and the complicity of the stepfather. Follow-up interviews with the authorities substantiated the abuse claims.

As extreme as this story sounds, it did happen. It opened my eyes as to the possibility of schoolchildren being exposed to traumatic psychological and emotional pain. You need to be aware of how that might manifest itself in your classroom.

## Keep Things in Perspective.

You've had a glimpse of some aberrant student behaviors, but just remember that most kids are well-adjusted. In a normal thirty-year teaching career, you may come in contact with close to a thousand children. The vast majority of these students will find a spot in your heart as you recollect their special talents, their comical antics, their kind words, and their endearing personalities.

## CHAPTER 6

# Range of Abilities in the Classroom

*People are just as wonderful as sunsets if I can let them be. I don't try to control a sunset. I watch it with awe as it unfolds, and I like myself best when appreciating the unfolding of a life.*

—Carl R. Rogers

You'll be in for a jolt when a picture emerges of the varying ability levels found in your classroom. Children are as different in their brain power as they are in their personalities. The range can vary significantly among a group of twenty or thirty students.

For example, in one fourth-grade class, I had a student, Samantha, reading at a seventh-grade level. She was also a gifted writer, producing stories and poems worthy of publishing. In every subject, she excelled. She mastered every concept instantaneously and challenged me to find ways of keeping her motivated and engaged.

At the same time, there was Kalem, who couldn't count without using base ten blocks. He slowly plowed his way through preprimer books. Writing a simple sentence was not in his repertoire.

Gone are the days when you could teach to an average- or midrange ability group, hoping that the low- and the high-level students would come along for the ride.

## Differentiated Instruction

So what are you supposed to do to meet them where they're at?

The answer lies in differentiated instruction. This is not a program or a toolkit but rather a form of instruction that encompasses the big idea—all students can learn at their readiness level.

Differentiated instruction embraces the goal of reaching high-level students, those who struggle, second-language learners, disabled students, and emotionally or psychologically handicapped kids, all while still maintaining a vibrant learning experience for the average learners. It can be implemented in every curricular area.

> ### Get Up Close and Personal!

Whether your students are above, at, or below grade level, it is essential to tap into their personal interests in order to motivate them. You'll turn a bored, apathetic student into an enthusiastic learner by delving into his world.

For instance, let's return to Samantha.

Once she declared her fascination with ancient Greek culture, I challenged her to research and share her knowledge with the class. She used every resource available and independently wrote a historical fiction with a Greek setting. That's the kind of student she was! My taking only a few extra minutes of the day to discover her interests opened the floodgates to her creativity.

You may want to eat lunch in the cafeteria with your students occasionally. I did this once a week, and we discussed favorite movies, music, games, etc. They didn't know it, but I used these conversations to design lessons to capture their attention throughout the year. When kids know you are interested in what their world is all about, they will respond with enthusiasm.

For example, Dane was a fourth grader, incapable of working independently. I needed at least one authentic writing sample from him for assessment purposes. I couldn't get him to write anything. He'd put his hood over his head like a turtle crawling into its shell and shut down.

I happened to be having lunch with Dane and other students one day when he became quite animated as he spoke about his *Star Wars* video game. I quickly discerned that *this* was his passion.

Thinking of him the next day, it popped into my head that the writing prompt would be "Write about your favorite video game." Dane's eyes lit up, and the pencil flew across the paper. It wasn't long before he had completed the assignment. The grin upon his face spoke volumes about his pride in his accomplishment.

What are some of the other things you can do to reach your students? Keep abreast of current music, popular television shows and movies, new toys, and technology. They'll be impressed with how comfortable you are in their realm.

Veteran teacher Carolyn Ayres was my role model to learn how effectively differentiated instruction could be used. She shared her story about Donny, one of the most gifted students in her teaching career.

"Donny was a constant problem in my second-grade classroom," Carolyn recalled. "He did not get along with the other children and was constantly causing a disturbance! He was the very worst during lessons where I engaged the whole class. Frankly, he was bored. He was one of the brightest children I ever had.

"When I'd finally reached the end of my rope, I began thinking about Donny as an individual. Seeing the world from his viewpoint, I came up with an idea," she continued.

"I asked the principal for a half day to create a special program for Donny. Although he could read well and was very good with math, his real interest was in science.

"I spent the first of my three hours laying out possible science readings and projects. The second hour, I invited Donny's mother to sit with me and choose from these groupings the things she thought he might like. The last hour, I had him join us and choose from things his mother and I had gone over. Included was a math book full of games that required critical thinking. I put together a binder of science readings and projects, and I asked that Donny also read the directions and learn to play three or four of the math games.

"I made arrangements to go over his work with him at least once a week to keep him on track and motivated. Donny was given a special corner in the room, shut off from the view of the class. He was invited to retreat to his spot when I was teaching things that he already understood well.

"As I suspected, the rest of the class realized how unique he was and had no problem with this special treatment. When a child finished his/her work early, he/she was welcome to go to Donny's corner to learn one of the math games.

"The peacefulness in the classroom was immediate. On the first rainy-day recess, I saw four children crowded around his desk learning and playing one of the games. Donny, who never had any friends, was now the center of attention!

"I vowed always to remember, a class is made up of individual children. It is my job not only to work with the class as a whole but also to respond to the uniqueness of each child."

## Multiple Intelligences

It's hard to talk about reaching all students without addressing the multiple intelligences of people as defined by cognitive psychologist, author, and professor of Harvard University's Graduate School of Education, Howard Gardner. He defined the first seven intelligences in his book *Frames of Mind* and added two more in *Intelligence Reframed*.

They are as follows:

- Verbal-Linguistic
- Mathematical-Logical
- Musical-Rhythmic
- Visual-Spatial
- Bodily-Kinesthetic
- Interpersonal
- Intrapersonal
- Naturalist
- Existential[1]

According to Gardner, all people possess all nine intelligences in varying amounts. And each person has a different intellectual composition or some combination of the various intelligences.[2]

I had one master teacher who taught from the assumption that all students could benefit from lessons geared to each of these specific intelligences. He incorporated lessons of each modality a certain number of times each week in his first-grade class.

For example, he used word walls, pictures with words, and key vocabulary and phonics flashcards for the young visual learners.

At the same time, he reached auditory learners by clapping syllables, repeating phonemes, and listening to recorded stories.

With a little creativity, various modalities can be adapted for use in any curricular area.

## Modalities in Math

The year I taught fourth grade, students had a particularly hard time understanding and using the "order of operations" in algebra. I challenged them to take the rules and make a song out of them. Two of my students were able to write lyrics about the "order of operations" sung to the tune of "Rudolph the Red- Nosed Reindeer." The buttons popped off their shirts when they read the lyrics and the whole class learned their song. These students were struggling in math, and they were so proud, they shared their song with the principal and the secretary of our school. All the students mastered this mathematical concept that year.

The takeaway? Take advantage of chanting and singing for teaching math concepts and basic facts.

In addition to this kind of musical/rhythmic stimulation, mathematics instruction also lends itself to using kinesthetic and tactile-based strategies. Math games and puzzles work well and reinforce mathematical reasoning. There are many online resources for you to choose from, and many are free.

Tactile learners need experiences with math manipulatives appropriate to their grade level.

For example, kindergartners can count out little plastic bears to internalize the number sense of counting. Intermediate-grade students may use rubber bands and geoboards to gain a concrete understanding of angles, area, perimeter, or finding the hypotenuse of a triangle.

My students get excited when I incorporate kinesthetic strategies when teaching angles. Third- and fourth-graders love getting up out of their seats, standing up, and stretching their arms out to show right, obtuse, and acute angles. By using their gross motor skills, their brains integrate these math concepts for better recall, and they have fun doing it.

Wait until you see thirty-two fourth graders jumping, turning, and spinning 45, 90, 180, and 360 degrees on command! By using skateboarding terminology that they are already familiar with, you will help them master an otherwise difficult math concept. You are essentially just renaming terminology—translating skateboarding jargon into rotational geometry.

This is a perfect example of reaching students with the bodily-kinesthetic intelligence. Have fun with this!

Would you like to reach your tactile learners? Try using small dry-erase boards for math—it's one of my favorites.

For example, after your students have been given a few minutes to solve a math problem, say, "Show me!" Then they raise their whiteboards up in the air to show you their work. You are essentially getting an instant assessment. You'll see immediately who has mastered the concept and who needs individual help.

## Modalities in Language Arts

The very young kinesthetic learners will benefit by using whiteboards to write words or phonemes. Clapping syllables in a spelling or vocabulary lesson will also engage these children.

Incorporate songs and videos into your lessons to tap into the auditory, visual, and kinesthetic intelligences to help students learn parts of speech, sentence structure, grammar principles, and so much more. This also works with math lessons. Some of my favorite musicians/teachers that I have relied on to get my students up singing, dancing, and learning are Ron Brown, Heidi Butkus, and Jack Hartmann. You can find their work online. You will find Ron Brown's products (songs for teachers and children) at intelli-tunes.com. Heidi Butkus has many beginning reading and math skills songs with fun movements. Go to heidisongs.com. Finally, Jack Hartmann's "Super Fun Learning Songs" can be found at jackhartmann.com.

One of the best programs for teaching reading that incorporates visual and auditory stimuli is John Shefelbine's SIPPS (Systematic Instruction in Phonemic Awareness, Phonics, and Sight Words). This program is a compilation of fast-paced lessons for teaching word-recognition strategies. In a short twenty-minute lesson, students learn to recognize words and syllables. They respond by orally chanting sight syllables and by reading entire words.

I was among a large group of teachers to see John Shefelbine speak at a conference. Our district supplied training and resources to implement the program district wide. I immediately began using it with my fourth-grade students. It generated a lot of enthusiasm and, in my opinion, significantly boosted their reading skills.

So does it work? Five hundred forty-seven students in California participated in a study on the effectiveness of SIPPS. Across all classrooms, students fared better in decoding on a normed assessment test. Additionally, English-language learners (ELL) improved even faster than English-speaking students. Assessments were given in the fall and the spring after seven months of instruction. High school students, who were also part of this research project, demonstrated significant gains using the SIPPS program.[3]

## Visual Intelligence in Writing

When I first started teaching writing, I had the good fortune of attending a "Step Up to Writing" workshop. It became the cornerstone of my writing program.

*Step Up to Writing* author Maureen E. Auman draws upon multisensory techniques to help students organize their ideas before they write. By using color-coded strips, students learn to write cohesive paragraphs in many genres.[4]

For example, before I knew the program, I had the students draw pictures only *after* their writing was complete. I had it backward! I thought the reward of drawing would motivate them to finish their writing. However, after using "Sketch to Stretch" from

*Step Up to Writing*, I learned that letting them draw the pictures *first* helped them organize their writing.[5] Sketching is one tool that helps visual learners jump start ideas for narrative, expository, or poetic writing.[6]

First, students sketch the beginning, middle, and ending plan for their writing.

For example, my second-language learner, Miguel, wanted to write about the time he was bitten by a dog. His first picture was that of a cute boy petting a dog. The second picture was of a howling boy with lots of tears, blood flowing, and a dog baring enormous fangs. His last picture was being cradled in the arms of his father, with his hand bandaged. The dog was in a cage.

The next step for Miguel was to put key words next to each illustration. Now, armed with the vocabulary to paint the picture, he was excited to write his hair-raising story!

You'll find that students who usually hesitate to put words on paper will leap into the sketching enthusiastically. It lays a firm foundation for the writing process.

Pictures also work well when teaching specific grammar lessons. When I teach homophones, I ask students to draw a quick picture next to the word. For example, they draw a sailboat next to *sail* and a five-cent symbol next to *sale*. They might draw a luscious pear next to *pear* and two socks next to *pair*. Simple drawings actuate the brains of the visual learners.

## Kinesthetic Strategies in Writing

Second-grade teacher Mrs. Walton uses a creative approach for reaching her kinesthetic learners. She uses traditional letter signs from American Sign Language for teaching high frequency words and weekly spelling words.

"My students hold their hand above their heads while they spell the words in sign language," she explained. "It's terrific!"

In primary grades you may want to make handwriting practice more interesting and engage the tactile learners by bringing out a can of shaving cream and squeezing a bit onto their desks or tables. Students take pride in showing you their carefully formed letters. They freely experiment knowing one swipe of the hand creates a new slate.

A time-management word of caution: This lesson can easily spiral out of control, so do set some parameters.

For example, students may only use one hand at a time, and if the shaving cream is found anywhere but on that one hand, their session is over. This may sound harsh, but take it from me, who learned the hard way, it **is necessary**! If they follow the rules, they get bonus time to free draw!

When you are done with the shaving cream, have them use damp paper towels to clean off their desktops. Voilà! Desks or tabletops are squeaky clean!

## Effective Strategies for Teaching Second-Language Learners

Obviously, vocabulary building is essential to students learning the English language. You'll want to use copious amounts of pictures, photographs, illustrations, etc. You don't have to be a Michelangelo to convey meaning with your simple sketches. Kids appreciate any attempt you make to clarify concepts in a visual mode. Have some fun and allow them to take turns being the artists.

When teaching vocabulary, ask your students if they have any understanding of the words being discussed. Check their prior knowledge. Next, teach word meaning *explicitly* and choose words that they will encounter often. Teaching words in context is more valuable than teaching an isolated word with a dictionary definition.

For example, you may come across a sentence such as this: "Father commended Gary for receiving a trophy at the soccer tournament."

A student could glean the interpretation that to be commended is a desirable action by the way the word is used in context. On the other hand, the word "commended" on a discreet spelling list would have no meaning.

For a more comprehensive study of vocabulary building strategies that are researched based, pick up a copy of *Bringing Words to Life: Robust Vocabulary Instruction* by Isabel L. Beck, Margaret G. McKeown, and Linda Kucan.[7]

Visual aids, such as pie charts, story maps, Venn diagrams, etc., help *all* of your students organize information and gain comprehension of the content area that you are teaching. These important graphic organizers truly help the second-language learners, and there's a smorgasbord of websites and books from which to glean your favorites.

Other techniques that will help these students are gestures, body language, and hands-on lessons.

Using photographs or 3-D objects ("realia") will help students who are acquiring the English language. Depending on your artistic skills, drawing beautiful illustrations or simply sketching stick figures will help all of your visual learners to understand difficult concepts.

My favorite use of realia took place around Thanksgiving. I dusted off a small wicker cornucopia that I picked up at a garage sale as my students prepared to read stories in class that made a reference to the "horn of plenty."

"I know what that is!" exclaimed one child. "My grandma puts it on her table every Thanksgiving!"

It's a powerful tool, and I knew that this vocabulary word, "cornucopia," would stick with those who needed the visual support.

On another occasion, we were reading a story about the famous hat maker, Stetson, from the Old West. I brought in a genuine felt Stetson hat to show my class. I was astonished to learn that many students were unfamiliar with felt!

As you can see, realia is useful in many settings. My students were captivated when I shared a quail nest complete with a few unhatched eggs during a science lesson.

When teaching science, building physical models is a concrete way of engaging second-language learners. They *will* enjoy making models of the solar system, the structure of DNA, a cell, an atom, etc. The ideas are endless.

English-language learners are often lacking in prior knowledge in many content areas. Be sure to provide the scaffolding they need to process the content of your lessons. If all else fails, heed this advice from one of my administrators: "Google a picture!"

What makes teaching interesting is also what makes it so challenging. Finding the strategies to fit with each individual student's learning style is like putting together a jigsaw puzzle. When you search for those pieces, it can be frustrating; however, when you hit upon the correct fit, it's enormously fulfilling.

**You're Thinking:** *I'll never be able to meet all their individual needs.*

**Your Need to Tell Yourself:** *I need to remember the old saying "How do you eat an elephant? One bite at a time." I'll find the best strategy for one child at a time.*

## CHAPTER 7

# Lesson Planning, Homework, and Report Cards

*If you are planning for a year, sow rice. If you are planning for a decade, plant trees. If you are planning for a lifetime, educate people.*

—Chinese Proverb

Your job as a teacher is multifaceted, but the lion's share is lesson planning and evaluating and assessing student work.

## Lesson Planning

You may work for a district which gives you a pacing guide for each subject, detailing the scope and sequence of your lessons and suggesting a date by which the topics should be covered. This is very useful in planning your lessons.

While it is human nature to procrastinate, the pacing guide will help you stay on track. If your district doesn't provide a pacing guide for lesson planning, you may want to collaborate with a grade-level partner and create your own. Also, find out if your district has a mentoring program. He/she can help you with this task as well. Be proactive and recruit a mentor at your school if one is not provided. Mentors offer a myriad of other supports such as navigating through school policies and procedures as well as simply being a good listener.

The pacing guide is more like a compass than a road map. It keeps you heading in generally the right direction, but be ready to make changes as needed.

Lesson Planning: Be Flexible!

You need to be flexible because things will develop that detour your best-laid plans.

Often, a lesson that you thought would take one day ends up taking three days. Or every teacher has the lesson that just doesn't land and must be retaught. You'll want to "spiral" and review concepts throughout the school year. Remember, coverage isn't the goal. (See "Mastery versus Coverage" in chapter 8.)

I remember when my teaching colleague, a brand-new teacher, was excited about having her lessons planned in great detail for the whole year. I couldn't quite find the words to tell her that she should be prepared to adjust and change her lessons as the year evolved.

"Teaching is never static," veteran teacher Jackie Evans explained. "When I first started teaching, I labored over detailed lessons plans, only to have them fall apart during the rest of the school week.

"One day, thankfully, early in my career, I realized that I could go ahead and make my plans but then enjoy how they twisted, turned, and changed. Then I relaxed and enjoyed the process."

You'll soon feel comfortable with your weekly lesson planning, but it's imperative to regularly lift your head up and take a wide-angle view of the trimester and even the calendar year. Make sure you are prepared for all the forthcoming activities and holidays.

For example, every year I took my class on a field trip to the National Coleman Fish Hatchery in Anderson, California. I needed to look at the horizon and prepare several science lessons on the life cycle of the salmon prior to the trip. I also planned an art project to complement the science lessons.

Covering your entire curriculum is similar to making your way through a tantalizing smorgasbord, realizing that your eating capacity is limited. Even though it all looks good and you want to sample it all, you realize you must survey your choices and determine what will satisfy you. Likewise, in the classroom, you won't be able to serve up the essentials if you feel compelled to partake of everything!

The most common lament you'll hear from a teacher these days is "There's just not enough time to teach everything!"

One of the most calm, centered teachers I have ever met gave me this advice. She told me to make a list of all the things that I wanted to teach. The list naturally fell into a hierarchy of importance. I took her advice and scheduled the most essential lessons daily (math and reading). Next, I included the less urgent lessons once every other week. This helped assure me that I would eventually teach a variety of subjects to my students.

It's a satisfying feeling to touch upon things like poetry and creative writing which are too easily overlooked.

**You're Thinking:** *This is frustrating, I am not keeping up with the pace! There's not enough time in the day!*

**You Need to Tell Yourself:** *Focus on skills and understanding. I'm going to be flexible with pacing and lesson planning.*

## Homework

Find out what your school or district's policy is regarding homework. Your district may have a "no homework" policy. Or some districts may even have guidelines for homework broken down by grade level (K–8) with daily minutes recommended.

Assuming that your school does recommend homework, let parents know that it is an opportunity for reinforced learning at home. Stress that it should not become a point of contention. Homework fosters deep feelings, both pro and con. Some parents complain that their students aren't receiving *enough* homework, and others declare they are getting too *much*. Ask parents, teachers, and students their opinions on this subject and you'll receive a wide array of answers.

Opponents believe that homework puts undue stress on students. They contend that homework is ineffective. Also, there are concerns about how much time is spent doing work at home.

Proponents believe that homework can reinforce classroom learning. It helps children develop personal responsibility, good study habits, and time-management skills. For me, personally, looking over the completed homework gave me the opportunity to reteach concepts that students missed. While the other students worked independently, I could pull those students back to give them the extra instruction they needed to master the concept.

The important question is: "How much homework is the right amount?"

> ## Make Homework Purposeful!

As a new teacher, you may want to rely on the simple ten-minute rule. Add ten minutes of homework for each grade level. For example, a third grader would receive about thirty minutes each night.

In *Classroom Instruction That Works*, by Robert J. Marzano, Debra Pickering, and Jane E. Pollock, the authors present teachers with four generalizations to guide them in the use of homework. They are

1.  The amount of homework assigned to students should be different from elementary to middle school to high school.

2.  Parent involvement in homework should be kept to a minimum.

3.  The purpose of homework should be identified and articulated.

4.  If homework is assigned, it should be commented on.[1]

## Weekly versus Daily Homework

If you've decided to assign homework, will you go with daily or weekly? Each teacher has his or her own preference. You'll have to decide which system works best for you and fits the type of families you serve.

After going back and forth for the first few years, I found there were positives and negatives with each. A friend of mine polled parents of a few primary classes to determine their preference. These comments were copied verbatim from the survey sheets:

### In Favor of Daily

66 *[It] helps my child get in a daily routine.*

66 *I feel it really helps their homework skills. Weekly packets make students too relaxed. They put the homework off 'til the last minute.*

### In Favor of Weekly

66 *When we have soccer games during the week, it's nice to know we have the weekend to do it.*

66 *To be honest, it don't matter to me if it's weekly or daily. I make my son do it no matter what. (And that's my favorite quote, by the way!)*

## Report Cards

Your district will more than likely dictate what your report card will look like. In turn, your report card will dictate what type of record-keeping system you'll need to implement.

Take advantage of the technology that's out there to save you time. There are many software programs for grading. These can help you facilitate this important part of the teaching job.

Discretionary sections on report cards may include student learning behaviors and/or teacher comments. Most parents appreciate teacher commentaries and are eager to read the heartfelt observations about their child.

As a parent of three kids who attended public schools, I looked forward to reading a sentence or two that encapsulated the essence of my child's school experience.

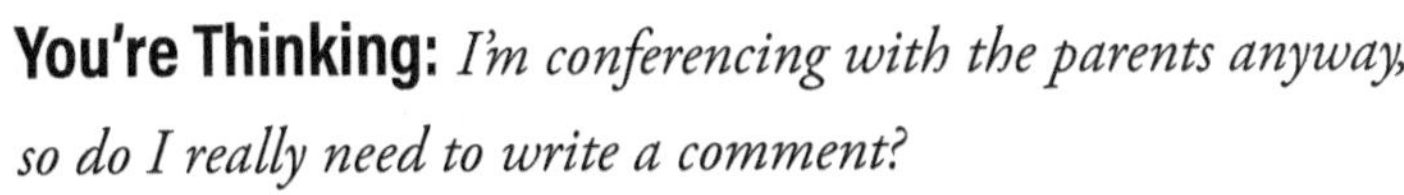

**You're Thinking:** *I'm conferencing with the parents anyway, so do I really need to write a comment?*

**You Need to Tell Yourself:** *What I write is a lasting record that will be valued by the parents and the student.*

Lesson planning, homework management, and completing report cards are the underpinnings of a teacher's duties. Each year you will refine your system until these responsibilities become effortless.

## CHAPTER 8

# Nuts and Bolts: Curriculum and Philosophies

Within the nitty gritty of teaching—curriculum trends and teaching philosophies—there is always one thing you can count on: ***change***. You will repeatedly hear the phrase "the pendulum swings . . ." as you mingle with veteran teachers. However, it's not always the philosophy that changes. Teaching methods come in and go out of style. Sometimes it's just a name change.

## Staying in Step with Terminology: Direct Instruction or Explicit Instruction

I found myself at a district training session when the discussion turned to "Explicit Instruction." I had the feeling of déjà vu all over again. I remembered that my instructor in credentialing school taught this as "Direct Instruction."

So, I thought to myself, *What's the difference?*

I asked the presenter to clarify the distinction between the two and she couldn't!

After doing my own research, I discovered that researchers, writers, and publishers seem to be using the terms synonymously.

Yet to change the terminology of such a well-entrenched teaching method seemed counterproductive to me. Let's examine this further.

Direct Instruction has a well-documented history and a clear and concise definition. Professor and researcher Siegfried Engelmann formalized the logic and methods for Direct Instruction in the late 1960s. He aimed at finding special instructional methods that would enhance the learning of children and young adults. He is considered the architect of Direct Instruction.[1]

## The Tenants of Direct Instruction

- **Setting a Purpose for Learning**—The teacher shares the objectives and procedures for learning the new task, activating prior knowledge and connecting to previous lessons.

- **Teacher Presentation**—The teacher tells students what to do and explains, demonstrates, or gives examples of the skill or strategy.

- **The "Watch Me" Part**—This is a modeling and highly structured practice. The teacher leads students through the lesson, in a step-by-step fashion, often with the use of visual aids.

- **The "We Do It" Part**—Providing guided practice, the teacher gives students the opportunity to work on their own with help and support.

- **The "You Do It" Part**—As an independent practice, the teacher allows students to practice completely on their own until independence is attained.[2]

You will want to familiarize yourself with the components of Direct Instruction because it lends itself to any curricular subject across all grade levels and reaches all ability groups.

Large- and small-scale studies have been done to show that Direct Instruction is unique in its positive effects on student learning. I can attest to this after seeing the significant gains my students made each year.

**Direct Instruction Lesson**

Language Arts Lesson Plan

The Setting of a Story

**Setting a Purpose for Learning (Objective)**

Students will understand what the setting of a story is.

**Teacher Presentation**

The teacher begins by telling the students that the "setting" of a story is the *when* and *where* its plot or action takes place.

**Sequence of the Lesson—"Watch Me"**
*(This is the presentation part.)*

First, the teacher chooses a picture book that the students are familiar with. She states, "In this book we know that the farmer lives in the country on a farm. We also know that it is summer because the trees have leaves on them." This is the setting: a farm in summer.

For older students, she refers to a chapter book that she's been using for a read aloud. "In this book, we see that the action takes place in New York City. We also know that it is winter because the sky is gray and snow piles are everywhere." The setting is New York City in the winter.

Continued...

**"We Do It"**
*(This is the guided-practice part.)*

The teacher asks for volunteers to tell the others the title of the book they are reading. Each student is asked to state what the setting of the story is—naming the *when* and the *where*.

The teacher continues with the "We Do It" part, calling on different students, until she/he feels comfortable that the class understands the concept of setting.

**"You Do It"**
*(This is the independent practice part.)*

The students are placed in small groups (three or four). The teacher asks the kids to select a book they are reading and describe the setting to their "elbow partner" or the students in their group.

The teacher walks around the room listening to their conversations while checking for understanding (informal assessment).

## Safeguarding Instructional Minutes

There has to be cohesion between the quantity of actual minutes spent in instruction and the quality of instruction during those minutes according to the authors of *Delivering on the Promise of the 95% Reading and Math Goals.*[3]

In chapter 2, Principal Dave Montague of Washington Elementary School explained, "Start twenty minutes late or stop twenty minutes early and do that every day during first, second, and third grade, and your students lose the equivalent of an hour daily of direct reading instruction during their first three years."[4]

At Montague's school, the 120 minutes of the reading block are inviolate. According to this administrator, "Direct Instruction is becoming an art form in our school. Minute for minute we use it perhaps twice as effectively as we did five to eight years ago."[5]

Many states have strict grade-level standards which dictate what teachers are supposed to teach and what students are expected to learn. The adopted curriculum is closely aligned to these requirements.

When I started teaching, the curriculum was saturated with standards-based pedagogy. Having no prior experience, I embraced it fully.

However, once I entered the classroom, I could see the veteran teachers struggling to abandon their prior curriculum. They were low on Direct Instruction and high on thematic units, games, etc.

The key is striking a balance. You can employ engaging strategies based on *standards* which puts parameters on *what* you teach, not *how* you teach. You can make learning fun!

> The Fusion of Teaching the Standards
> with Direct Instruction Equals Success.

## Mastery versus Coverage

Circumstances required that I go on a personal leave for several months at the beginning of one school year. A long-term substitute teacher was contracted for this time period.

Miss Littlejohn appeared to cover the curriculum at breakneck speed. My grade-level partner at the time, Connie, would occasionally call and inform me that she couldn't keep up with the frenzied pace of Miss Littlejohn. Connie would tell me, "I've given her my lesson plans for the week, but she comes to me wanting more after two days!" She had those kids zipping through the lessons!

Judging by the end of the trimester assessments, she may indeed have been covering the material, but the students weren't mastering the curriculum.

Harry and Rosemary Wong state in their book *The First Days of School*:

> Teaching is not covering chapters or assigning activities. Do not become enamored with presenting information, doing activities, and using the technology present in the classroom. Nothing is being achieved if there is no evidence that students are actually learning the lesson outcomes or objectives. The purpose of school is learning.

Teaching is not what you do to fill up a day. Teaching is the outcome you get from students.

Learning has nothing to do with what the TEACHER COVERS. Learning has to do with what the STUDENT ACCOMPLISHES.[6]

Wong continues:

Success is achieved when teachers write lessons with crystal clear objectives and precise instructions so that students understand what the outcome or result of the lesson will be.[7]

[Permission: Harry K. Wong and Rosemary T. Wong, *The First Days of School: How to Be an Effective Teacher*, 5th ed. (Mountain View, CA: Harry K. Wong Publications).]

Let's look at this scenario of Mrs. Castillo teaching a language arts lesson to her third graders.

She exposed the students to the basic elements of a story ***once*** (plot-problem and solution, characters, setting, and theme). She asked them to memorize the terms, and then said, "Your assignment is to read a short story and be prepared to name the elements of this fiction story on Friday's test."

In this situation, the objective was to learn the basic story elements. Before the students can be assessed, however, the teacher must present numerous lessons and examples from the literature they are familiar with. This might come from whole group discussions of what they are reading in class, from the books they are reading individually, or even movies they have seen.

Be realistic: You can't expect students to grasp any concept with the first presentation of the lesson. Students need to hear it or be exposed to it multiple times.

I have heard that students need to hear the idea/concept anywhere from sixteen to forty times in order to retain it. It's worth repeating that repetition is *important*. Even after the concept has been mastered, it's crucial to spiral your teaching, that is, revisit it throughout the year in order to keep those ideas fresh in their minds.

As a new teacher, don't ask what you will cover tomorrow, this week, or this month. Instead, ask yourself, "What do I want my students to learn, accomplish, or master?" Then design your lessons with clear-cut objectives in mind.

Think of yourself as a mason. You're building a brick wall with that first important lesson. Every time you reteach the concept it's like adding mortar and bricks to allow for further construction. The finished wall represents a concept mastered.

## Reaching the Whole Group: Student Engagement

How can you be sure that you are getting through to all of your students at their unique cognitive level? Here are some of the engagement strategies that I have used whole group with success.

### *Choral Response*

Teachers use "choral responses" instinctively.

For example, my math lesson objective was counting money using quarters. I asked my students to chant "Twenty-five cents, fifty cents, seventy-five cents, a dollar."

By varying the groups of students doing the chanting, you keep them all on their toes (boys wearing white T-shirts, girls with long hair, kids wearing tennis shoes, etc.)

## Partner Response

Partner response (elbow partners) is effective with any subject you teach. You will like using this with your writing assignments.

For example, give your students a couple minutes to talk to their partners about the topic "A Favorite Summer Activity." This generates ideas for their writing.

Pairs work well together during writing activities and other lessons. Ask each student to tell you what their partner said. This not only gets their creative ideas going but also helps to develop good listening skills.

## Written Response

Graphic organizers are a gold mine in assisting students to organize their thoughts and, therefore, comprehend what they read. There are more examples of graphic organizers than you can use in a lifetime, so be discerning.

Many scholars will point out that certain written responses elicit greater gains in comprehension than others. Three separate studies conducted by Marzano (1998); Marzano, Gaddy, and Dean (2000); and Marzano, Pickering, and Pollack (2001) showed that some of the instructional strategies that produce the largest percentile gains in student achievement are identifying similarities, differences, note-taking, and summarizing.[8]

It is clear that summarizing information and comparing and contrasting (whether in a matrix, table, or Venn diagram) is proven to be the most effective. Students learn to recognize signal words like "same or different" and "in contrast to" when doing comparison writing.

## Individual Response

The first hands thrown in the air in response to your question aren't necessarily indicative of those students who have the right answer. In fact, you will soon notice that many students put their hands up before you have completed asking the question. Therefore, fight the natural inclination to call on those first few students. There are more efficient ways of eliciting individual responses.

For example, "wait time" is a valuable technique which aids students in accessing information stored in their long-term memory and brings it back to short-term conscious memory. Retrieving information is a cognitive task: It takes time (three to five seconds) for their brains to work! This wait time may seem unnatural. Surprisingly, most teachers only wait an average of 0.7 to 1.5 seconds before permitting a response.[9]

It takes practice, but the payoff is big. You'll get more quality answers. The "no" and "I don't know" answers decrease. When you use this wait time with your students, encourage them to preserve the three seconds of silence as well.

Another way to elicit individual response is to draw names to determine who will answer the question. Student names can be on sticks, cards, or just about anything. This allows even the most reluctant student to have the opportunity to respond. It fosters engagement. Everyone must be prepared to respond.

One of my favorite comprehension strategies is a game I created called "King of the Hill." I used it with the whole group.

After a short reading assignment (expository text works well), the students are responsible for creating their own written test questions about the passage. They must be able to give the correct answer and be able to prove what part of the reading passage the answer came from. One student is selected to be the King or Queen of the Hill. Students take turns trying to stump the King using their own questions. The King continues to reign as long as he answers correctly. When the King makes an error, the person who asked the question that stumped the King then becomes the heir to the throne. The students soon realize that the more questions they formulate, the better their chance to become the King or Queen.

> Education Is Ever Changing.

## Be Open to New Ideas

In education, change is the norm. Some changes are subtle while others are monumental. Sometimes the change is in the ***how*** of teaching, whereas other times, the change is in the ***what***.

As an example, let's look at the pedagogy of language arts. At one time, whole language was the favored trend. Teachers embraced a less structured, more holistic approach to teaching language arts. Now, however, whole language has been largely abandoned and replaced with an explicit, systematic method of teaching phonics and decoding words.

It's really more important to find your own personal teaching style than to let prevailing trends dictate your approach.

## Curriculum in the Classroom

I was fortunate to have books on the shelves my first year of teaching, but I knew teachers who weren't so lucky and had to scramble from room to room to obtain reading materials for their students.

Many school districts work in conjunction with the state when it comes to new curriculum adoptions. It can change as frequently as every five to seven years.

You may discover that some teachers are as reluctant to give up their old, familiar curriculum as Grandpa is to part with his comfortable, worn-out recliner.

Be willing to fully embrace a new program in order to fairly assess its effectiveness. You can always adapt it later to meet your specific needs. I am reluctant to pass judgment on a program that I haven't fully taught in the way it was designed. Give it your best shot, then you are qualified to critique it.

If the opportunity arises to be part of a curriculum adoption committee, take it! Not only does it give you a voice in selecting the soon-to-be-adopted materials, but it also gives you a preview of what to expect once the adoption is made.

Since computers and technology play such a big part in education, you will want to familiarize yourself with whatever it is that your school district has to offer.

Your district is going to adopt and purchase the license to use a variety of computer programs. In addition, there are numerous free programs and apps that you will want to explore. Students love the new technology, so use it to its fullest capabilities.

**You're Thinking:** *Oh, I finally mastered this new reading curriculum! I am set!*

**You Need to Tell Yourself:** *I need to remember that the program could change next year, and I need to be flexible. One thing is certain: it will change routinely.*

Be flexible with your attitude toward your curriculum. Rest assured that the instructional strategies outlined in this chapter could be adapted to any curriculum. Be confident and keep learning.

## The Importance of Professional Development

Whether you're a newbie, a second stager, or a veteran, you'll want to take advantage of any seminars, workshops, or professional-development programs that come your way. But that's not ***enough***!

While we think of professional development as workshops and seminars, what experts in the field are finding is that peer coaching and professional learning communities (PLCs) make the biggest impact in changing thinking and enhancing the teaching experience.

Mike Schmoker gives us a clear picture of what these learning communities look like in the book *On Common Ground, The Power of Professional Learning Communities*. He states, "It starts with a group of teachers who meet regularly as a team to identify essential and valued student learning . . ."[10]

The team collaborates to create lessons, share strategies, set achievement goals, and develop assessments. Teachers in PLCs shift the focus. They adopt the philosophy of "we, not me." Learning from each other becomes a routine practice.

Observing peers at your own school is an excellent way to learn new techniques and establish networks for support. It is especially helpful if you can collaborate with your grade-level partner(s). Your confidence and skills will improve as you connect with your colleagues.

At my school, the administrator provided an opportunity for teachers to observe each other several times a year.

Marcy Newman, a California middle school teacher said, "During the last three years that we've had PLCs, I've had more interaction with more people in more departments than in all my other twenty-three years of teaching here put together."

Teachers come together regularly to ask these critical questions: What is it that we want students to learn? How will we know when they've learned it? What happens when students have trouble learning it?

How can teachers then judge how effective this kind of collaboration is?

They judge their successes on the basis of results. They work together to develop common standards-based assessments and use these to drive their instruction. They adopt the practice of assessing *for* learning, not *of* learning (see *Student-Involved Classroom Assessment* by Richard Stiggins).[11]

> ## The Fusion of Teaching the Standards with Direct Instruction Equals Success.

So what are the payoffs of PLCs?

- Boosts professional morale
- Greater job satisfaction
- Higher retention rates
- Student learning soars
- Higher achievement results

Rarely does the research community come together in such a unanimous way as they do in support of PLCs. It cannot be denied that this kind of continuous, professional collaboration pays off in a big way to students and educators.

In this vein, extensive research has been done at the Harvard Graduate School of Education. It is called The Project on the Next Generation of Teachers (PNGT). It focuses on issues facing teachers in their second stage of teaching (years four through ten). The study paints a picture of a group of competent educators who value their independence but feel they are adrift with no guidance as to how they can expand their expertise.

One PNGT study examined districts which offered educators opportunities for collaborative development. They found that collaborative "professional learning helped the teachers remain confident and satisfied in their current commitment to teaching."[12]

*New* educators, like yourself, want to grow as professionals. But it's tough to do it alone. Rely on your colleagues as well as your administrator for professional guidance.

## CHAPTER 9

# Assessments and Accountability

*You teach. Kids learn. You test. Kids perform. Get comfortable with testing; it's an integral part of teaching.*

—Source Unknown

As a new teacher, I was quite surprised by the quantity of state and district testing that was required. Along with this came the formidable amount of pressure of achieving high test scores. Everyone in education—your superintendent, your principal, and even you, yourself—has a stake in racking up high test scores.

## Formal Assessments and Student Buy-In

You've done the teaching. Now it's time for the students to *show what they know*!

There are a lot of state and federal tests that must be administered. You want your students to have the *desire* to do well and have a vested interest in demonstrating what they have learned.

So how do you go about doing this?

Set goals and provide feedback.

## Students Set Goals

I used the Accelerated Reader (AR) program since my first year of teaching. I loved it! And the kids loved it too!

This online program gives students the opportunity to set goals for their independent reading. The best part is that kids can take short quizzes after reading a book to check to see if they've understood it (comprehension). Students receive immediate feedback on how well they did, and they earn points. Teachers use these quizzes to track each student's progress and set appropriate goals for each.[1]

AR encourages kids to read at their own level and pace. The idea is for students to enjoy reading! They can select books that interest them—fiction or nonfiction. There are thousands of titles to choose from on its Bookfinder® list.[2]

The students in my class often asked for "more silent reading time" so they could meet their goal. Those who met their goal were rewarded with a movie party held in the gym every trimester. It was a super motivator! A lot of teachers had their own rewards and prizes: pizza, ice cream, popcorn parties, extra playtime outside, etc.

## Providing Feedback

A very important component of student accountability is to provide feedback on a regular basis. The importance of giving feedback cannot be understated. It's been my experience that when students are given the opportunity to set goals and correct, review, and revise their work, buy-in results.

For example, I gave chapter assessments for our school's adopted math curriculum. Before I started a new unit, I returned the corrected math tests along with red felt pens to the students. I reviewed and explained each problem while the students self-corrected. They *love* red pens! This was a quick review, but it also provided a springboard for the new unit.

**You're Thinking:** *I really want my kids to perform well on the upcoming state test.*

**You Need to Tell Yourself:** *My kids will do well if I have them set goals and provide them with feedback on their performance all year long.*

Author Richard Stiggins, in his book *Student-Involved Classroom Assessment,* contends that the goal of each student must be to become competent, not merely beating others' scores. The teacher's goal should be to instill in the students the belief that success is within reach if they keep trying. It's a great confidence builder.[3]

Stiggins differentiates between assessments *of* learning versus assessments *for* learning. Assessments of learning ask if students are passing externally imposed tests (state, district, etc.). Assessments for learning are more diagnostic for the purpose of practice and improvement. He states, "One is for accountability, while the other is intended to support learning."[4] He outlines the teacher's role in assessments for learning:

- The teacher must clearly understand the standard to be mastered.

- Break it down into individual classroom achievement targets, leading up to overall goal mastery.

- Involve the students in creating a kid-friendly version of the targets for learning.

- Give only the highest quality assessments of the targets.

- Use these assessments in tandem with the students to track achievement over time.[5]

## Support Your Students through Informal Assessments

You will be evaluating your students using informal assessments as well. These include classroom discussions, individual questions, worksheets, pop quizzes, projects, reports, journals, writing portfolios, etc. All the information you glean from these assessments will be the fuel that powers your instructional decision-making.

## Building Accountability

Embedding accountability into your classroom is an ongoing refining process that yields great dividends.

My year-long mantra was "Take charge of your own learning." It was *so* satisfying to have a student parrot that thought back to me.

For example, before our timed multiplication test, Lance excitedly announced, "I took charge of my own learning last night. I reviewed my times eights for twenty minutes."

Of course, it was no surprise when Lance aced the test.

## Ticket to Lunch

An easy method for motivating your students and holding them accountable is with the "ticket to lunch" incentive. It can be used for any written assignment that needs completion.

For example, I used something called "sentence surgery" for teaching grammar. Write an error-riddled sentence on the board (with incorrect punctuation marks, spelling, grammar usage, etc.). Then students copy their corrected version on their papers. Next, they take turns coming up to correct the errors on the board while those at their seats are expected to make the changes that they missed the first time. Students clamor to be the one at the front of the classroom.

I became frustrated when I walked around and saw that several students never bothered to make the corrections on their paper. The solution was something called "a ticket to lunch." I told my students that I would hold them accountable for the completed assignment at lunchtime. Once students realized that their place in the lunch line depended on how fastidiously they corrected their sentence, the quality of the work went through the roof.

It's important to note that I didn't use a canned program for the daily grammar lesson. The students looked forward to seeing sentences that were related to their own school experiences.

For example, when I taught proper nouns, commas, homophones, etc., I included a few students' names in a sentence such as: *jessica, mitch, and clint sat next to there teacher at the veterans day assembly.* The authentic sentences provided a hook.

Jessica, Mitch, and Clint sat next to their teacher at the Veterans Day Assembly.

## Accountability and Homework

When it comes to homework, my belief is that it is important. I had a high return rate on homework assignments largely due to the fact that the students knew that I would check it in and hold them accountable if it was not turned in.

Early in my career, the teacher next door came to me asking, "Can I use your trash can to throw away these papers? I never have time to correct homework, and I don't want my students to see that I've thrown it away."

She disposed of the students' homework all year long.

My philosophy is simple: if the homework doesn't warrant me assessing **how** they've done it, then it isn't worth their time *or* mine to assign it at all. It doesn't take long for students (at any grade level) to perceive that their work is not valued. Kids know when their work is disregarded, and the product becomes increasingly subpar. Remember, students can discern whether or not you are looking at their work.

## Visual Feedback

As teachers, we hold ourselves accountable by testing and assessing student mastery of concepts throughout the year.

Visual reminders in the form of sticker charts or bar graphs can be displayed on classroom walls to bring students into the loop of accountability. Often teachers use student numbers rather than names to ensure anonymity. Filled with pride, students receive gratification when they see their progress highlighted. Kids get excited about how much they've learned when they see the continual ascent of colored bars, line graphs, sparkly stickers, etc.

> It's All about Students
> Taking Charge of Their Own Learning.

If you're a parent, you'll know that the most common reply to the question "What did you learn in school today?" is "*Nothing.*"

If you're a teacher, you know that your students just spent the last six hours learning everything from order of operations to understanding metaphors.

I know one teacher who asks her students at the end of the day to take out their journals and quickly jot down one thing they learned today that could be shared with their family. It's a self-reflective time that conveys several ideas: learning is important and valued, excitement can be generated about learning, and the teacher cares about their learning and so should they.

This metacognitive process ("thinking about thinking") plays a critical role in successful learning. What you're really hoping for, in the long run, is that students are learning how to become lifelong learners.

## CHAPTER 10

# Parents:
# Friend or Foe?

*At the end of the day, the most overwhelming key to a child's success is the positive involvement of parents.*

—Jane D. Hull

Now that you have a good idea of how to teach, what to teach, how to assess, and who the students are that you're reaching, it's time to consider the parent/teacher relationship. You'll be communicating with many parents, so it's important to keep it positive and professional.

What should you expect? Sure, you will have parents who bring you Starbucks coffee and dark chocolates on Valentine's Day. But how will you deal with the ones who barge through your door to cuss you out in frustration?

Here are some stories that will help you deal with these parents and other scenarios that are even more thought provoking.

Of course, the overwhelming majority of parents are nice folks. Usually, you'll encounter adults at the beginning of the school year who want to volunteer. They generally help in the classroom, chaperone field trips, participate in parent clubs, help with fundraisers, support athletic boosters, etc. It is something to be encouraged at all levels.

It's tempting to want helpers in your classroom as soon as possible; however, consider a few things first before saying yes. Here is the question you will need to ask: What are their motives? While parents can be the greatest of allies, they can inadvertently present obstacles to your teaching.

**You're Thinking:** *Sign up every able-bodied adult for classroom volunteers.*

**You Need to Ask Yourself:** *What are their motives for wanting to be in the classroom?*

## The Observer

Many parents will want to come into your classroom to get a feel for your style and to see how well it meshes with their child's personality. In other words, "What's this teacher like?" and "Is Melissa going to be happy and comfortable in this classroom?"

They may want to observe the class dynamic to satisfy themselves that you have good control as the teacher and are able to promote an atmosphere of learning.

Although these are admirable motives, and indeed qualities of an involved parent, you may want to exercise caution in what duties you assign **this** type of parent.

In general, these parents don't consistently come to the classroom beyond the first month or two.

Shelby's mother, Mrs. Morrow, approached me on the first day of school.

"What can I do to help you? I'd like to come every week and help out."

"Great!" I replied.

I set it up for Mrs. Morrow to help every Tuesday and Thursday morning with a new P.E. program I was expected to implement. With twenty-five students in my third-grade class, an extra pair of eyes and a whistle around the neck meant I could be more effective teaching sports skills.

It was wonderful. Mrs. Morrow showed up consistently twice a week for all of September. It was like having a mini sports camp every session. I watched with satisfaction as my students developed their soccer skills. Mrs. Morrow was an essential part of their success.

Having come to rely upon this responsible parent, I planned to teach basketball skills the following month. Here again, I knew that small group instruction would be more manageable and students would be better able to stay focused with two adults supervising.

*Rin-n-n-g-g!* I picked up the phone in the classroom. Mrs. Morrow was expressing her regrets.

"I'm sorry, I can't make it today. My dentist is fitting me in for some crown work. I really need to have this done," she said.

"No problem," I answered. "See you on Thursday."

This was the first example of what was to become a pattern of excuses. Her twice-weekly help dwindled to once a week, then once a month, to once in a blue moon.

When the "observation period" is over, and parents are satisfied that their child is functioning well, they seem to volunteer less and less or not at all. In other words, these are not the parents to put in charge of long-term projects, reading or math groups, or anything requiring a consistent, time-intensive commitment.

So what do you do with these short-term parent volunteers? By all means, take advantage of their involvement while it lasts. Just be sure that what you assign them can easily be finished by someone else (an aide, another parent, or yourself). Possible tasks may be filing, preparing art projects, checking in homework, listening to a child read, correcting papers, etc.

## Helicopter Parents

If the "observing" parent could be considered a "concerned" parent in a healthy sense, then the "helicopter" or "enabling" parent is an unhealthy extension of a concerned parent.

The coined term "helicopter parent" effectively conveys the idea of the parent who hovers over their child to a stifling degree.

These are parents who unintentionally instill feelings of helplessness in their children. Because Mom or Dad (or both) have overseen every little thing the child has done their whole life (or has actually done it for them), the child begins to get the message that they are incapable of doing it for themselves.

For example, my fourth-grade student, Cody, was noticeably obese. Mom walked him into my classroom, carrying his backpack and an adult-sized lunch pail. She hung up his coat, sat down next to him, and began coaching him with his schoolwork. She did this for about two hours each day.

Eventually, I felt that I had to address this situation with his mom. After our conversation, she shortened her stay, but because of the ingrained coddling, Cody expected my undivided attention for the rest of the day. He was unable to produce any work without prompting. Despite my best efforts, it was difficult to nurture any seed of self-reliance in Cody.

# GROUNDING THE HELICOPTER PARENT

Do your student a favor by rerouting his/her helicopter parent. With tact, you may convince the parent that the child needs to experience independence in school.

Another example of this would be Javier, a bright, although immature, student. His mother was the quintessential helicopter parent.

"Has Javier turned in his homework?" she would ask at the end of every school day. "How is he doing on his writing assignment that you started today?"

I quickly realized that I had to be careful about how I reported his performance. Anything less than a sterling report resulted in a verbal berating from mother to son.

She showed up to help at our Christmas party. To Javier's dismay, she began coaching him on how to win the mystery gift of our party game.

Sitting in a circle, the players pass around an elaborately wrapped gift. When the music stops, the person holding the gift frantically tears away at the wrapping paper. The gift must again be passed around as the music resumes. The winner is the person who removes the *final* layer of gift wrap.

It was enormous fun for everyone except Javier. I noticed tears welling up in his eyes as he handed off the wrapped present at lightning speed after the initial embarrassment of Mom's "helpful hints."

## Volunteers May Surprise You

One grandmother surprised me when she came into my classroom to learn. She came regularly and would cheerfully complete small tasks quickly and efficiently. She also had a flair for art.

However, when I asked her to correct a multiplication test (using a key), I realized it was more work to go back and correct the mistakes she made rather than do it myself.

One day she shared the fact that she had failed miserably in math and was fearful that she had passed "those bad math genes" onto her granddaughter. I then began to notice that anytime I was teaching a math concept, she was totally absorbed in my lesson. I learned that if I *really* needed her help in completing something on a given day that I could ask her to take the project out into the hallway where she could complete it without being disturbed.

I tried as much as I could to balance those days with the days where she could just sit as a student and master those elusive fractions. Now she had the confidence to go home and tutor her granddaughter.

## Competitive Parent

There is a positive correlation between student success and parent involvement. Logic would say that it could only be a boon to the teacher to have parents that are highly interested and involved in their child's education. However, just as a healthy concern can be taken to the unhealthy extreme of becoming a helicopter parent, it can also mutate into something equally negative when that "concern" is motivated by a "competitive spirit."

For example, I remember thinking how nice it was that my master teacher, Mrs. Finch, was able to enlist two responsible parents to help with reading groups twice a week. The kids reaped great benefits from the extra support.

However, there was one parent whose primary motivation for being there was to see that her son, Garrett, maintained his status as the top reader in his second-grade class. To her chagrin, she discovered that Alyssa was reading a full level above Garrett on the computerized program used for the students' independent reading.

I was standing nearby when I heard this mother ask, "I noticed that Alyssa's book level was higher than Garrett's. Are you sure that he's reading at the right level?"

Without missing a beat, Mrs. Finch replied, "Well let's just be sure. Why don't we have Garrett stay after school and retest on the computer?"

Mrs. Finch saved her words knowing full well that the test results were recent and accurate. She had had enough experience to know that this parent needed to *see* the results in black and white. Naturally, the test results were identical to the first.

These parents not only scrutinize their child's performance but they also thoroughly examine everything the teacher does.

**Projecting Perfection Takes Its Toll!**

Poor Mrs. Finch! She was meticulous to an extreme, trying so hard to please an abundance of these types of parents. To her horror, she noticed a mistake in the homework that had gone home that day.

My inclination would have been to let it go and, perhaps, include an apology in the next day's homework. She, on the other hand, insisted that it was necessary to call all twenty parents the minute school was out, before any of the parents discovered the error.

Bear in mind that Mrs. Finch was a highly respected and experienced teacher. When I offered to help her so that the task could be completed in half the time, she declined. She felt it required her *personal* apology.

You can imagine my humiliation a few days later when she was put in a position to apologize to a parent for *my* mistake! I had marked one math problem wrong on a homework assignment. Perfection was at a premium when it came to handling "perfect" parents. She promised the parent she would have a heart-to-heart talk with her student teacher about the transgression. Looking back, I am grateful that only *one* parent called to complain.

**You're Thinking:** *Everything has to be impeccable!*

**You Need to Tell Yourself:** *Mistakes will happen—they are essential to the human learning experience.*

Mrs. Benedict had over twenty years of experience at fifth grade, teaching in both affluent and economically disadvantaged schools. She was so good that many of the teachers in this school district put their own children in her class. At one point, she had the children of seven teachers and one principal in her room.

One day at lunch, she announced, "I can't take this fishbowl atmosphere any longer!" Teachers in the lunchroom were shocked as Mrs. Benedict continued, "My transfer was approved. I'll be teaching fifth grade at Green Oaks next year."

The school she transferred to, Green Oaks, had one of the highest percentages of students on the free or reduced school lunch program. She came to this decision largely due to the pressures put upon her by the competitive parents. It was a decision she never regretted.

## Irate and Problem Parents

Because parents of schoolchildren are just people, and life is often problematic, all of the difficult and even scary situations imaginable can and do happen.

I had just finished a parent-teacher conference with Mr. and Mrs. Lane. Their daughter, Amber, received a stellar report card.

They started to leave when Amber's dad turned to me and said, "May I have a word with you alone?"

"Sure," I replied.

Once his wife left the room, Mr. Lane launched into an attack that left me dumbfounded!

"This is the most despicable, disgusting report card, and I won't accept this!"

He questioned why Amber didn't receive *all* "outstanding" marks for behavior. I tried to justify my "satisfactory" marks by saying, "This is only the first trimester, and I like to leave room for improvement."

He replied, "You're implying that my daughter isn't perfect. She has *never* received a report card with anything less than outstanding."

Had this been an ordinary conversation, I'm sure we could have found some common ground. However, it was apparent that this man was irrational. He stood inches from my face, waving the report card in the air, and yelling, "You *will* make the changes. I will not accept this."

This experience left me speechless and shaken to the point of tears. It took me some time to reclaim my usual confident demeanor.

This was the beginning of several threatening encounters I had with this man. This situation put a serious strain on the relationship I had with his daughter. It forced me to walk on eggshells around her. His overly zealous protection of his daughter had instilled in her a heightened sense of privilege and superiority. I've always taken pride in treating my students with fairness and respect, however, I'll admit I went out of my way to appease Amber in order to avoid Dad's wrath.

It was disconcerting to me to realize that this might not be an isolated incident. Within weeks, my grade-level partner, Elena, had her own experience with an irate parent that left several of her students in tears.

She had recently received an email from the principal, Mr. Bean. He advised her not to let Sandy's father take her out of school. There were custody issues, and she was not to leave campus with him.

Elena was in the middle of a read aloud when Sandy's father came bursting through the door.

"Get your backpack, Sandy. We have to go. Right now!" he said emphatically.

His booming voice startled the children.

Elena quickly positioned herself between Sandy and her father.

"No you're not. Not without clearance from the office!"

Sandy's dad was a tree trimmer by trade.

"I just saw my boss falling from a tree. He could be dead," he answered dramatically, "I need to get to the hospital."

Although he seemed genuinely distraught, it crossed Elena's mind that this could be a ploy. Custody issues are so emotionally charged!

She tried to appease him, "That may be. But you still have to sign her out at the office."

"This is bullshit," he yelled, picking up Sandy's backpack and slamming it to the floor. He turned to his daughter, "Get your things, we're leaving."

Almost miraculously, Elena spotted the principal walking past her window.

"There's Mr. Bean. Get his okay and you can take her," she told the belligerent father.

Fortunately, he took her advice. She quickly locked her doors and gathered her class on the carpet, like a hen gathering her chicks.

Some children were still crying. All were noticeably upset. One of them voiced the thoughts of all the students. In a shaky voice he said, "Teacher, he can't talk to you like that."

Elena calmed them down by grabbing their favorite book. In contrast to her churning emotions, she did her best to read in a calm, soothing tone.

It was no surprise when Elena found out a few months later that Sandy's dad was in jail for other issues.

**Don't Go It Alone!**

Whether you're a brand-new teacher, or you've been in the classroom for twenty years, these are the kinds of parents you are going to see. How are you going to handle them?

Conflict is inevitable. When you're facing irate parents, realize that help is nearby. The previous year's teacher, your grade-level teachers, and, most importantly, your administrator all make great sounding boards.

For example, after the angry Mr. Lane had left campus, I needed to regain my composure. On my way to the restroom to wipe away my tears, I met up with Mrs. Simpson, the teacher who had trouble with him last year.

She consoled me by saying, "He has no right to treat you that way. He's scary, and I thought he was going to hit me when I was alone with him in the classroom. Our administrator stepped in and ordered a legal restraining order."

Later that week, I met with my administrator, who agreed to mediate any future conferences with the Lanes.

Because of this experience, the following year, I was well equipped to handle an irate and irrational parent who accused me of "child abuse" during a parent conference. She questioned my practice of having disruptive students miss part of their recess.

Sensing her emotional instability, I immediately suggested we continue the meeting with my administrator present. It was quickly resolved with the support of my administrator. I felt like a professional instead of a punching bag this time around.

Sometimes, however, there may **not** be colleagues or administrators on the site to help you. Sixth-grade teacher Ms. Kelly was left alone at the end of the day with a threatening parent.

"In spite of the inconsequential nature of the issue (missing homework), the boy's father was furious," Ms. Kelly recalled. "He yelled and screamed in my face for several minutes, unwilling to let me talk. Then he stormed out of the classroom and stood in the schoolyard, without leaving campus. Despite locking my door, I still felt vulnerable. I picked up the phone and called the police."

These are true case scenarios. Be cautious and professional in dealing with parents knowing that some may be unhinged.

## Gems

It only takes one or two encounters with problematic parents to make you want to say no to volunteers. Fight that urge! Here's why.

I came across a parent, Mrs. Bosworth, who became more like a colleague than a parent. She did accounting work four days a week and approached me about the possibility of volunteering an hour or two on Fridays.

Here was a parent who obviously had great organizational skills. I could depend on her to be in my classroom once a week to correct papers, work with small groups of students, or monitor the class while I pulled students for remediation. She did *whatever* I asked, quickly and efficiently.

Mrs. Bosworth was one of those parents who understood immediately what I wanted, without a lot of direction. She was intuitive about knowing what needed to be done.

In addition, she would always keep our classroom treasure box full of prizes and jump in to purchase any needed supplies for the students.

Parents like Mrs. Bosworth counterbalance the high-maintenance parents, like those described earlier. It doesn't take long to recognize competence and reliability. Once parents present themselves as someone you can depend on, scoop them up! These are the true gems!

> ## Involved Parents Are a Precious Commodity!

It's indisputable that parents who interact in the educational experience will have students who perform better academically, have better attendance, exhibit increased motivation, and improve their self-esteem. Negatives will be diminished. Suspension rates drop as do the incidences of drug and alcohol abuse.

Do get your parents involved in their students' education. It pays big dividends!

## CHAPTER 11

# School Climate

In the past, parents assumed that schools were safe places for their kids. Today, however, metal detectors greet students at high-risk schools. Many now have "zero tolerance toward violence" policies in place. Words like "lockdown" or "intruder alert" are part of the school vernacular because of the horrific, tragic shootings that have infiltrated our culture and seem to be proliferating.

If there is any danger posed at your school, be ready to follow the procedures and drills. You are the students' first line of defense. It is imperative that you learn the safety guidelines specific to your school site. Report any unsafe situation to your administrator *immediately*.

One school used the code words "Bring the trophy to the office" to signify a lockdown. This triggered a well-practiced sequence of events designed to protect students and staff. The staff knew immediately what actions to take without alerting the intruder.

I recall a lockdown at my school. It was about 3:00 p.m. when I heard police sirens coming closer. The students had gone home, but a few after-school programs were still in session. Then I heard the code words on the intercom telling us we were in lockdown. I locked my doors and crawled under my desk.

As I later found out, it was more than a drill. The police were in pursuit of someone who had just held up a nearby convenience store. They apprehended the fleeing suspect as he ran across our campus.

## What's a Teacher to Do?

The big question is "Why are these situations so prevalent in our schools today, and what can we do about it?"

The answer is complicated. Undoubtedly, drug and alcohol abuse, unstable home lives, poverty, mental illness, and the influence of media are some factors that foster violence. Countless hours spent in front of computers or video games designed to maim or kill imaginary enemies are suspect.

For example, I had one third-grade student who would suddenly make very unusual hand movements in the middle of a lesson. In a trance with his eyes crossed, his pistol shooting fingers battled invisible forces at a frenetic pace. This happened several times a day. I asked his counselor to see if he could solve the mystery of Dylan's bizarre behavior.

The counselor was very pleased with himself when he came to me with the full explanation. "Dylan is imagining himself in the throes of his video game when he is making those strange motions," he said.

When I brought this up with Dylan's mother, she admitted it was his *addiction*.

Video games, TV, the internet, music, movies, etc., *do* influence children. These are things that you have little or no control over; therefore, focus on things you can control.

## Controlling Your Classroom Atmosphere

Keep in mind that you can control your classroom climate. Reassure your students that they are in a safe environment. Establish good communication and talk openly about issues with students and their parents.

In my district, we have several programs designed to teach interpersonal skills. They include anti-bullying, problem solving, character education, and more. Be sure to find out what program your school and/or district implements.

In my classroom, I had the Golden Rule poster hanging on the wall. We talked about what it means to be "a Golden Rule class."

It meant, of course, that we treated each other the way we wanted to be treated.

I took advantage of the misunderstandings, hurt feelings, name calling, etc., to discuss how we might resolve these issues by making them see the situation from the other student's perspective. When appropriate, I used the time as a whole class teaching moment, reinforcing the principles that we advocated as a class. Whether it was through class discussions or role-playing, I found that with time, the students reminded each other how to respond in the "Golden Rule sort of way."

Your goal is to ensure every child is treated respectfully and feels safe in your classroom.

## Opinion and Politics in Public Schools: What's Appropriate?

*A teacher affects eternity; he can never tell where his influence stops.*

—Henry Adams

As a new teacher, you will face many controversial topics, whether it's an upcoming national presidential election or a closer-to-home, hot-button issue. You will have your opinions, it's true, but you also have great power and influence. What you say in the classroom or in your community matters. It's a good idea to remain objective as you teach and discuss current events. Keep partisan politics out of the classroom.

**You're Thinking:** *It would be fun to talk to my students about who I voted for and why.*

**You Need to Tell Yourself:** If *I discuss politics, I need to be objective and present both sides.*

## Shaping Students' Lives with Life's Lessons

*Teaching kids to count is fine,*
*but teaching them what counts is best.*

—Bob Talbert

One of the most rewarding aspects of teaching is character education. It is surprising how receptive students are during spontaneous discussions about compassion, honesty, empathy, perseverance, integrity, responsibility, respect, etc.

Students are like sponges. They are thirsty for these life lessons. In some cases, school is the *only* place they will learn these principles.

These character-education moments take place naturally. They happen in everyday interactions with your students. No need to schedule time in your plan book. These lessons truly are *caught*, not taught, and you have to take advantage of the authentic circumstances of the moment.

I remember once when the phone rang during class time. I was keenly aware that the students were eavesdropping as I apologized profusely to another teacher. I had completely forgotten to include Mrs. Donnely's class when making a reservation for the field trip to the fish hatchery. There was no way to fix the problem. Her students simply would not be able to go. I felt terrible, and, after hanging up the phone, I noticed how intensely the children had been listening to my conversation.

I used this as the perfect teaching moment. I turned to the class and said, "You see, even teachers make mistakes. Maybe you guys can help me think of a way to make it up to Mrs. Donnely's class."

"I know," Isabella exclaimed, "Let's have a pizza party and invite them!"

"Great idea," I said as I immediately put the plan into motion by reserving the cafeteria for the upcoming Friday afternoon.

Whether it's a miscalculation during a math lesson or a misunderstanding with a colleague, students are usually surprised when teachers err. It's okay for students to see your mistakes as long as you model an open and honest way to rectify the situation. It's a learning experience for all.

**You're Thinking:** *I wouldn't dare let the kids know that I can't spell "judgment." I'll quickly think of a synonym to write on the board.*

**You Need to Tell Yourself:** *My class needs to see that I'm not perfect. I'll ask them to help me check the correct spelling.*

Instilling values, morals, and ethics in children is a solemn charge but reaps great results and satisfaction.

I had a poster in my classroom titled "Student's Bill of Rights." It lists statements like "I have a right to be heard," "I have a right to feel safe," "I have a right to be respected regardless of the color of my skin," etc. I referred to this poster whenever a student felt slighted or disrespected.

I told my students, "You are part of a school family." I taught the words "empathy" and "compassion" and what it really means when we say, "We care about each other's feelings. We solve problems and stand up for each other."

They knew they were safe, loved, and respected in my classroom. Absolutely "no bullies allowed"!

Look how Jackie Evans created a nurturing environment that transformed the life of one of her students.

"Chad was a strange child," she explained. "His mother was into voodoo. He was angry and withdrawn.

"One day he threw a chair, and it hit me! I sent him to the principal. He was suspended. When he returned a few days later, I asked him if he could explain his behavior. Tears welled up in his eyes as he confided, 'I have no friends.'

"I asked if he would like to have a class meeting to talk about his concerns. He must have trusted that this would be a positive experience because he said yes."

Jackie continued, "At the meeting, I asked for a show of hands as to how many students ever felt left out. Everyone raised their hands! We talked about making and keeping friends from a first-grade point of view. We brainstormed about how we could help

Chad. He seemed pleased since many of the children expressed how much they liked him and made an effort to include him.

"A few days later, we were doing an art project and someone made a picture for Chad. It started a domino effect, and many of his classmates joined in and made special creations dedicated to him. This proved that most everyone has a heart big enough to reach out to others."

> ## Make School a Student's Home Away from Home.

Every year the problem arises with students calling each other names or making fun of names.

We were just settling back down to work after lunch when Lucas came to me with red-rimmed eyes and declared, "Kids keep making fun of my name. They keep calling me 'Lucas Mucous.'"

I replied, "Did you use your words to tell them how you felt? Did you give them the 'I Message'"?

"Yes," Lucas whined, "but they wouldn't stop."

Before any lessons resumed, I used this opportunity to talk about respect to the entire class. Rather than have the culprits apologize, I thought it would be more effective to teach my students about empathy.

"Put yourself in Lucas's shoes," I told the class.

I asked someone to tell me how it would feel to be called hurtful names. They articulated very clearly how painful this would be.

I stated, "I won't ask 'Who did this?' but who can tell me what can be done to make Lucas feel better?"

Hands shot up.

"I think they should apologize," Elisa answered.

"That's one solution," I responded.

Then I picked up my shiny brass bell and rang it pointedly.

"While apologies are necessary, they don't take away all of the hurt. Unkind words are like ringing a bell. Once a bell has been rung, you can't unring it."

I could tell by their serious faces that the lesson had landed.

> **You Can't Unring the Bell!**

## The Eroding Image of a Teacher

As human beings, we hopefully learn from our mistakes and admit when we are wrong. Yet it's a reality: There are teachers with blurred lines of ethics and morality.

I've seen several examples of unethical behavior. One teacher came to school intoxicated while another had a sexual liaison on campus in the back seat of a car with the father of one of her students. I also worked with a teacher who ran a personal online business selling candy during class time.

Teacher misdeeds fall into two categories:—minor irregularities and serious misdemeanors and felonies.

Minor irregularities include making vacation reservations online during class time, leaving elementary students unattended to go run copies, etc.

Then there are serious misdemeanors and felonies: sexual misconduct with students, visiting pornographic sites online with students in the room, stealing money, furniture, computers, etc., from the school.

I worked with one teacher who stole money from another teacher's purse while she was out of the room. They were actually friends and grade-level partners. I later learned that she was a drug user and was arrested for passing fraudulent checks.

Then there was a former administrator of mine who had a heavy gambling problem. Something seemed odd to me at the time, but later it made sense. I had a bag full of bills and change that I collected from my third graders for an upcoming field trip. She saw me heading for the office to give the money to the secretary. She grabbed the bag of money and said, "I'm headed that way. I'll handle that for you." I later found out that the money never made it into my classroom account.

Stories like these and others may have a negative effect on the reputation of educators. There is growing public concern that unions make it difficult for school districts to get rid of bad teachers. In many cases, even the school districts turn a blind eye to the bad actors because of the fear of negative publicity in the community. However, an effective administrator will take action to remove the offending staff member just like a good surgeon removes a malignancy. Solutions to these situations are out of your control.

> **Don't Overstep Your Bounds!**
> **Let Your Administrator Do the Legwork!**

Steer clear of troublemakers and minimize their damage to your reputation. Surround yourself with honorable people. Seek out colleagues who are positive, professional, and enthusiastic. Remember, the overwhelming majority of teachers do have integrity. They love their students and put all of their energy into doing their best.

Most teachers are regarded as decent, venerable, and respectable people. With a reputation like this, there's no reason why we can't draw in the elite, quality, top-notch men and women into the field of education. It will take people, like *yourself*, to make a difference in the lives of children.

## CHAPTER 12

# Teaching from the Heart, Not the Book

*Fifty years from now it will not matter what kind of car you drove, what kind of house you lived in, how much you had in your bank account, or what your clothes looked like. But the world may be a little better because you were important in the life of a child.*

—Anonymous

It doesn't take a full year to realize that you are overworked and underpaid. It is imperative, then, that from the beginning, you consciously recognize and appreciate the genuine payoffs of teaching. Sure, you'll receive cartloads of love letters, cards, flowers, teacher cups, etc., but the rewards that truly matter are often subtle and can easily be overlooked or minimized.

Ask any seasoned teacher (whether still teaching or retired), "What are the joys of teaching?" That's exactly what I did, and this is what they said . . .

Phyllis Hutchinson taught kindergarten through third grade for fifty-three years in California. Her first year of teaching in Long Beach, she had thirty-eight morning kindergarten students, thirty-eight afternoon kindergarten students, and only sixteen chairs! It was a different era when Phyllis started her career in 1954. She can remember the momentous day when the superintendent gave the go ahead for female teachers to wear pants to school!

I've always admired Phyllis because she connected with each child individually. Also, she had a firm belief that to be an effective teacher, you had to include parents in the school experience.

"It goes beyond teaching," she said. "You have to reach out beyond the child and encompass the whole family. I was always so willing to plan the trips, (an annual field trip to San Francisco was just one example) and put on the programs (Patriotic Program, Clown Show, etc.) because I knew I would reap the rewards many times over. The parents became so active and supportive. I told new teachers, 'You have to put in the time and effort to get them (the parents) to school.'"

Phyllis also put in her own time, unpaid, before school and after school running her Reading and Science clubs.

"I had to arrange for the students' parents to bring them to school early for Reading Club or pick them up later in the afternoon for my Science Club.

"In the quiet morning hour, before school started, I would read with students one on one. I had five or more different students come every day. It was heaven! While I read with one individual, the other four kids would play games quietly on the floor.

"After school, a small group would join me one day a week, for one hour, to do hands-on science experiments. I didn't have time to do them during class, but these are the things that brought me personal satisfaction.

"Nevertheless, I realized early on that teachers need to have a full life outside of the classroom unrelated to school."

Many who didn't know Phyllis well thought teaching was her whole life. That wasn't true.

"I made it a point not to carry school home with me. I had my sorority and other activities my whole life. I encourage new teachers to find a diversion in order to avoid burnout."

Phyllis maintained the same energy, excitement, and enthusiasm for teaching right up until the year she retired.

## You're Going to Miss Them!

As the months flew by during the school year, I found myself becoming more and more attached to the children in my classroom. We did a daily calendar activity which showed days gone by and days to come.

With the days dwindling away, I said aloud, "Aww" to express my downhearted feelings. It was apparent that I touched the hearts of my students when they echoed back, "Aww."

## Self-Reflection

I think of teaching as a constant refining process. Often the one being refined is the teacher. The finest teachers are introspective and reflective about each teaching day.

My role model for this teaching quality was Carolyn Ayres, who taught primary grades for thirty-four years. She shared these thoughts.

"Every morning, I would remind myself, 'Be patient, kind, and loving.' However, as the teaching day progressed, I would hear myself being irritated or short with a child. I got to thinking that if a callous remark slipped from my mouth, maybe I could make amends afterward. What if I were to stop mid-moment and restate my thought in kindness? I decided to give it a try.

"My opportunity arose during a designated quiet time when a student I'd reminded a couple of times to whisper began laughing and disturbing those around him. I called him over and said (in an irritated voice), 'You've lost the privilege to sit with others.'

"The words had hardly left my tongue before I realized this was my chance to make amends. I quickly said, 'That didn't come out quite right. Can I try again?'

"He nodded.

"Then I said (kindly), 'What can I do to help you observe our quiet time?'"

"His attitude softened, and he said, 'I'll just take my book and sit over in the extra desk.'

"I thanked him, and the child smiled.

"Throughout the next few weeks, I continued to stop myself when I said something with a cranky voice. I would shift my attitude and rephrase my words. I was delighted with how it made me feel and with how the children responded to my kindness. This could be the end of the story, but it's not.

"During art period one day, I overheard Jocelynn bark out, 'Give me back my glue!'

"Almost immediately, she said, 'That didn't come out quite right. Can I try again?'

"She changed the expression on her face and said pleasantly, 'Can I please have my glue?'

"Jocelynn reminded me that my most effective teaching is done by *modeling* the behavior I want students to emulate."

## Why Do I Teach?

Veteran teacher Phillip Done explored the answer to this question in his award-winning book *32 Third Graders and One Class Bunny*:

"'No, come on, really,' said Natalie. 'Why did you become a teacher?'

"It was a good question—one I hadn't thought about since my student teaching days. I thought about it for the rest of the day . . .

"Why do I teach? Where else can you leave work and have hundreds of little people scream goodbye to you from the school bus every day?

"But the main reason I became a teacher is that I like being the first one to introduce kids to words and music and books and people and numbers and concepts and ideas that they have never heard about or thought about before . . .

"Just think about what you know today. You read. You write. You work with numbers. You solve problems. We take all these things for granted . . . There was a moment when you moved from not knowing to knowing. There was a moment when you moved from not understanding to understanding.

"That's why I became a teacher."[1]

## Have I Taught Them?

Phillip Done asks an even more important question than why he is a teacher. That is, what have they really learned? This comes from his chapter, "Have I Taught Them?"

"But have I taught them that it is better to tell me that they did not do their homework last night than to lie?

"Have I taught them that it is better to include someone in a four-square game than to tell him he cannot play?

"Have I taught them that Jefferson could not live without books, and neither can I?

"Have I taught them how to think when the answer is not right there in the text?

"Have I taught them that imagination really *is* more important than knowledge?

"Have I taught them that most of Thomas Edison's experiments did not work the first time either?"[2]

[From *32 Third Graders and One Class Bunny: Life Lessons from Teaching* by Phillip Done. Copyright 2005 by Phillip Done. Reprinted with the permission of Touchstone, a division of Simon & Schuster, Inc. All rights reserved.]

## Wait for the Payoff!

You don't have to teach for fifty years to cash in the dividends that teaching provides. Laurel Chee had this experience to share after her fourth year of teaching.

"Robert was a special boy," Laurel explained. "He is the reason I get up earlier than my body wants to and leave work later than my mind wants to. Robert is the reason I repeat instructions four times in a row eighteen times a day with a smile on my face. He is why I begin preparing my classroom in the summer, long before I am paid to be there. Robert is my inspiration because I never knew the *power* of teaching until I met him.

"Robert has Asperger's syndrome, a difficult disorder that makes social connections hard and fixations on subjects like fish or dinosaurs a daily battle. Although he was in my mainstream classroom, he had some very specific needs that made him more challenging to teach than my other students. He needed constant guidance to find and keep friendships, hourly reminders to maintain classroom routines, and language structures to connect to others and express his needs. Did I mention I also had to teach him how to read, write, add, and subtract?

"Fast forward to six weeks before the year was over: Robert *finally* figured out where to put his unfinished work. He turned to a neighbor and said, 'That was easy!'

"I turned my back to the class and pondered. I thought about the eight times a day I had reminded him that unfinished work goes in the red folder in his desk and how sad he had always looked because he couldn't remember that on his own.

"At the end of the year, when I passed out my students' writing portfolios, Robert looked up at me as I passed by his desk.

"'What do you think about your work?' I asked.

"'It's so funny,' he replied, 'I can do *so much* now!'

"The hug I got from Robert on the last day of school, coupled with his teary eyes as he thanked me for being his teacher, is enough to remind me year after year that I make a difference every day I go to work.

"Robert was a special boy, indeed—most notably because he showed me how special it is to be a teacher."

## Lunchroom Laughs

Now retired after a long teaching career (elementary and junior high), Patty Mullett relied on her own natural comedic abilities and her students' words and actions as the material to get the staff laughing at lunch. I always looked forward to her coming in with that look that said, "Have I got a good one for you!" Here's one that comes to mind.

Patty recounted her phone conversation with John's mother. This second grader was a challenging boy whose behavior warranted an almost daily phone call home during the teaching day.

When John's mom answered, Patty explained, "I told her that John wasn't turning in his work and that he's having a hard time paying attention in class. I said to her, 'I feel that these issues are hurting him!'

"John, who was standing near my desk and listening to the conversation, said quizzically, 'My shoes don't hurt!'"

Here's another one . . . A first-grade teacher at my school shared this at lunch one day: "I was finishing up my lesson on mammals. Josh, knowing that mammals had hair, said, 'Then my uncle is not a mammal!'"

More than likely, your school will have an anti-drug and alcohol program in the curriculum. This is what happened to Alice Cascarina in her Special Ed classroom.

"I noticed Elliot started coming to school with greasy hair," said Alice. "He was usually clean and well dressed.

"Hoping not to offend him, I mentioned that I took a shower every day.

"'How often do you take a shower?' I asked him."

"'Every day,' he answered.

"Then I asked, 'How often do you wash your hair?'"

"'Well, I used to do it every day,' he said, 'Now I still wash it every day, but I only use water.'"

"Then he leaned over and whispered, 'I looked at the ingredients . . . and it has *alcohol* in it!'"

"It's okay," I said as I held back a giggle, "as long as you don't drink your shampoo!"

## The Best Reward

This anecdote, written by Philip Krump, a fifth-grade teacher, shows how influential a teacher can be in the life of a child.

"Last year, I had an English-language learner in my class from an economically disadvantaged background. Nancy worked so hard in every subject. She took pride in her work and always wanted to present her best. She did this all the way up the grades so that by the time I had the privilege of teaching her in fifth grade, she was making consistently high marks. But it didn't come easily for her. She had to put extra effort into it.

"All year I was pulling for Nancy. I had this cheerleader inside saying, 'Yay, go, Nancy!' I started to say things to her in class like, 'So, Nancy, when you run for president, you'll have my vote!' Then I would say to those listening, 'She thinks I'm kidding.'

"We do these things as teachers. Just trying to get kids to dream big.

"In June, we awarded her Student of the Month because of all her hard work and increasing success. At the end of the year, I reminded her, 'Remember Nancy, when you run for president, you've got my vote.' Well Nancy (who is pretty shy normally) got up her courage, turned to me, and said, 'I don't want to be the president. I want to be a teacher.'

"I hate to cry in front of fifth graders."

## Parents Praise Teachers

I came across this lovely letter written by the parent of a first grader. She took the time to write to the local newspaper to express her gratitude toward one special teacher.

"The teacher simply hung the moon and stars for the children in her class and their parents. She blended the old-school fundamentals of excellence in reading, writing, and arithmetic with innovative programs that introduced her students to the geography and customs of places around the world.

"When I would ask my son what he did at school for the day, he always had volumes to say about the places he 'visited,' the words he learned to spell (like leprechaun), and so many other wonderful things.

"I would just like to acknowledge this wonderful teacher for getting it right and making a difference in our lives."

## To Be a Teacher

Harry K. Wong opens his book with a unique dedication to his parents:

> Dedicated to my father and mother, who wanted me to be a brain surgeon. I exceeded their expectations. I became a scholar and a teacher.[3]

He also includes a poem that all aspiring teachers will appreciate.

"Teaching"

A Poem by Harry Wong

The art of teaching is the art of assisting discovery.
You can teach a lesson for a day,
but if you teach curiosity, you teach for a lifetime.

It's too bad that the people who really know how
to run the country are busy teaching school.
When truth stands in your way,
you are headed in the wrong direction.
When teaching the love of truth,
never lose the truth of love.
Teachers' task: take a lot of live wires
and see that they are well-grounded.
The mediocre teacher tells, the good one explains,
the superior one shows, the great one inspires.
Nothing improves a child's hearing more than praise.[4]

[Permission: Harry K. Wong and Rosemary T. Wong, *The First Days of School: How to Be an Effective Teacher*, 3rd ed. (Mountain View, CA: Harry K. Wong Publications).]

## The "Ah-Ha!" Moments: Teaching Advice from a Veteran

Twenty-five-year veteran Jackie Evans shared these words of wisdom to rookies. However, her inspirational words will recharge any teacher whose bulb may be burning a bit dim.

- Plan your day, but know that no day will go as planned.

- Have the confidence to realize there's always a way to make the hard parts of teaching easier.

- Being open-minded makes for a happy teacher.

- You don't have to be an expert to teach any subject. I'm not an artist, but I teach art.

- Teaching—it's never boring. I've never had a second of boredom.

- You're a role model. If you're calm, confident, positive, and accepting, it transfers to kids.

- Keep a class photo every year. When your former students surprise you with a visit, you'll remember who they are.

I hope that these tips and tales from dedicated teachers remind you of why you wanted to become a teacher.

Your teaching career will be like a patchwork quilt. You're going to gather materials from teachers that have taken the journey of the noblest profession. You will take the fabric squares that appeal to you and stitch them together with the threads of your own personality and values.

The rewards of teaching are hard earned, but if you hang in there, you will not regret the time, sacrifice, and heart you invest.

Just remember . . . yours may be the name that is spoken when the question is asked: "Who was your favorite teacher?"

A Bb Cc
12345678
HAPPY
RETIREMENT
WE WILL MISS YOU!
#1 TEACHER

# References

## Chapter 2

1. American Institute of Stress, "Digesting the Statistics of Workplace Stress," https://www.stress.org/workplace-stress.

## Chapter 4

1. Harry K. and Rosemary T. Wong, *The First Days of School,* 3rd ed. (Mountain View, CA: Harry K. Wong Publications, 2004), 183.

2. Jim Fay and Foster W. Cline, *Parenting With Love and Logic* (Colorado Springs: Nav Press, 2020).

3. Jane Nelson, Lynn Lott, and Judy Arleen Glenn, *Positive Discipline in the Classroom* (New York: Three Rivers Press, 2013).

4. The Flippen Group, *Capturing Kids' Hearts* (College Station, TX: The Flippen Group Publications, 2005).

## Chapter 5

1. Centers for Disease Control and Prevention (CDC), "Fast Facts: Preventing Adverse Childhood Experiences," https://www.cdc.gov/violenceprevention/aces/fastfact.html.

2. Centers for Disease Control and Prevention (CDC), "Autism Spectrum Disorder (ASD)," https://www.cdc.gov/ncbddd/autism/index.html.

## Chapter 6

1. Howard Gardner, *Intelligence Reframed* (New York: Basic Books, an imprint of Hachette Book Group, 1999).

2. Gardner, *Intelligence.*

3. John Shefelbine and Katherine K. Newman, *Systematic Instruction in Phoneme Awareness, Phonics, and Sight Words,* (Alameda, CA: Developmental Studies Center – Center for the Collaborative Classsroom, 2001).

4. Maureen E. Auman, *Step Up To Writing,* (Dallas: Voyager Sopris Learning, 2016).

5. Auman, *Step Up.*

6. Auman, *Step Up.*

7. Isabel L. Beck, Margaret G. McKeown, and Linda Kucan, *Bringing Words to Life: Robust Vocabulary Instruction,* (New York: Guilford Press, 2013).

## Chapter 7

1. Robert J. Marzano, Debra J. Pickering, and Jane E. Pollack, *Classroom Instruction That Works,* (Alexandria, VA: ASCD, 2001).

## Chapter 8

1. Siegfried Engelmann and Douglas Carnine, *Theory of Instruction: Principles and Applications,* rev. ed. (Eugene, OR: NIFDI Press, 2016).

2. Englemann and Carnine, *Theory of Instruction.*

3. Lynn Fielding, Nancy Kerr, and Paul Rosier, *Delivering on the Promise of the 95% Reading and Math Goals,* (Kennewick, WA: The New Foundation Press, 2004).

4. Fielding, Kerr, and Rosier, *Delivering on the Promise.*

5. Fielding, Kerr, and Rosier, *Delivering on the Promise.*

6. Wong, Harry K. and Rosemary T., *The First Days of School.*

7. Wong, Harry K. and Rosemary T., *The First Days of School.*

8. Robert J. Marzano, Debra J. Pickering, and Jane E. Pollack, *Classroom Instruction That Works,* (Alexandria, VA: ASCD, 2001).

9. Mary Budd Rowe, "Wait Time: Slowing Down May Be a Way of Speeding Up!" *Journal of Teacher Education* 37, no.1 (January 1986): 43-50, https://doi.org/10.1177/002248718603700110.

10. Richard DuFour, Rebecca DuFour, and Robert Eaker, eds., *On Common Ground, The Power of Professional Learning Communities,* (Bloomington, IN: Solution Tree Press, 2005).

11. Richard J. Stiggins, *Student-Involved Classroom Assessment,* (Upper Saddle River, NJ: Merrill Prentice Hall, 2000.)

12. Harvard Graduate School of Education, "The Project on the Next Generation of Teachers," The President and Fellows of Harvard College, (Cambridge, MA: 1998), https://projectngt.gse.harvard.edu/.

## Chapter 9

1. Renaissance Learning, Accelerated Reader, https://renaissance.com.

2. Accelerated Reader, https://renaissance.com.

3. Stiggins, *Student-Involved Classroom Assessment.*

4. Stiggins, *Student-Involved Classroom Assessment.*

5. Stiggins, *Student-Involved Classroom Assessment.*

## Chapter 12

1. Phillip Done, *32 Third Graders and One Class Bunny,* (New York: Touchstone/Simon and Schuster, 2005), 249-–50.

2. Done, *32 Third Graders,* 283-84.

3. Wong, Harry K. and Rosemary T., *The First Days of School.*

4. Wong, Harry K. and Rosemary T., *The First Days of School,* 322.

# About the Author
# Janis Hawthorne

Janis Hawthorne has been involved in the educational community for many years both professionally and as a volunteer.

She was the recipient of the American Teaching Fellowship Award and graduated with honors from Simpson University in California.

Having taught elementary grades (K–4) for nearly twenty years in Northern California, she led curriculum development committees in her school district and served on School Site Councils.

Before teaching, she worked with young students as a mental health paraprofessional. It was one-on-one play therapy that helped these children acclimate to school. This experience gave her the life-changing epiphany that working with kids was the most rewarding thing she could do. That, along with encouragement from a terrific teacher and principal, gave her the impetus to become a teacher.

# About the Author
# Deborah Upshaw

Deborah Upshaw received her teaching credential from Humboldt State University in California and taught elementary school (K–4) for over twenty years in Northern California.

Prior to becoming an elementary school teacher, Upshaw had a successful fifteen-year career as a freelance writer, publishing more than two hundred articles in national and regional magazines. She shared her love of writing by teaching workshops to children and adults in her local community.

She shifted gears and began working with struggling readers as an aide in an elementary school. As her teaching skills grew, so did her students' reading abilities! That's when she knew that she wanted to become a teacher.

⚜

When the Hawthorne-Upshaw team aren't collaborating on a book project, you'll find them swinging their irons on the golf course!

www.ingramcontent.com/pod-product-compliance
Lightning Source LLC
Chambersburg PA
CBHW052028150726
48002CB00002B/510